The Three Sisters
INDIAN
COOKBOOK

For Aman
who truly believed in us

The Three Sisters
INDIAN
COOKBOOK

FLAVOURS AND SPICES OF INDIA

*Delicious, authentic,
easy recipes to make at home*

SEREENA, ALEXA & PRIYA KAUL

First published in Great Britain by
Simon and Schuster UK Ltd, 2010
A CBS Company

Text copyright © Abacus Publishing Limited
Design and new photography copyright © Simon
& Schuster UK Ltd

SIMON AND SCHUSTER
ILLUSTRATED BOOKS
Simon & Schuster UK
222 Gray's Inn Road
London WC1X 8HB
www.simonandschuster.co.uk

A CIP catalogue record of this book is available from the
British Library.

The right of Abacus Publishing Limited to be identified
as the Author of this Work has been asserted by them in
accordance with sections 77 and 78 of the Copyright,
Designs and Patents Act, 1988.

10 9 8 7 6 5 4 3 2

Editorial Director: Francine Lawrence
Managing Editor: Nicky Hill
Project Editor: Abi Waters
Design: Geoff Fennell and Joanna Macgregor
Production Manager: Katherine Thornton
New Photography: William Shaw
Home economist for new photography: Sara Lewis
Stylist for new photography: Liz Hippisley
Photographer and home economist for original
photography: Tim Hill and Zoe Hill

Colour reproduction by Dot Gradations Ltd, UK
Printed and bound in China

ISBN 978-0-85720-027-3

Recipe notes:
All teaspoons and tablespoons are level.
All spice spoons are rounded and 1 spice spoon is
equivalent to $\frac{1}{2}$ teaspoon.
All cooking times are approximate and will vary in
accordance with the type of cooker hob, conventional or
fan oven used.
As you familiarize yourself with the recipes, feel free to
experiment with the amount of chilli used to suit your taste.
Please be advised this book includes recipes where nuts
have been used.

A fun snap of us as teenagers taken in India. Alexa is posing,
Sereena's in the middle and Priya is standing.

Hamari Khanee

Our Story

Whenever we three sisters discussed Indian food, there was always a fourth person so fondly mentioned: our mother. She always took great interest in cooking for friends and family. Even the simplest home-cooked dishes had some small detail that would turn it into a special meal.

Our childhood was spent in the rich valley of Kashmir. The panoramic Himalayan scenery followed us in all directions; the clear sky and the mountain fresh water were the most memorable. We would play all day, building up a great hunger for a meal that would be almost ceremonial in its procedure. The six children in our extended family would be poised at every meal, cross-legged on the floor with such good discipline, waiting to be served. Until the rice, vegetables, meat and salad were all placed neatly on our thali (large steel plate), no one dared to start. And our meal was so delicious! Was it the fresh air, the water from the mountains rumoured to have digestive properties, or the fact that we had spent so much energy playing and were ready to eat when called? Whatever it was, Kashmir had, and still has a great mystical lure for us and our thoughts always go back to the Valley, which offered us so much throughout our childhood.

We founded our company Flavours & Spices on the premise of bringing this original flavour of India to Europe and America. We went to India searching Indian household kitchens, restaurants and snack bars for the authentic spices that flavour popular Indian foods and helped form our memories. Finally, our search led us to produce both this book and the Indian spice box, which can be bought ready-made or built up in your own home using our guidelines as to what to include (see pages 12–13).

Starting your journey

When we moved to the UK, we frequently entertained and cooked for our English friends. We would always be asked to cook an Indian meal as it was something that they would only occasionally do at home because it looked so difficult. We explained that it was straightforward as we used all the essential spices that were stored in our spice box (*masala dabba*), together with the required fresh ingredients.

However they did have a point; the recipes were stored in our heads, memorized from years spent watching our mother cook. This made us realize that if we could provide our friends with a spice box containing all of the relevant spices and a recipe book with step-by-step instructions on how to prepare and cook the recipes, then they could bring Indian cooking into their own homes.

We think the recipes provide the perfect mix, whether you want a quick snack for lunch, a tasty family meal or something a little more special for a dinner party. Almost all the spices you need will be in your spice box – whether you have bought it ready-made or created your own from scratch (see pages 12–13). Everything else you need to know is in the following pages, so you are now ready to start your journey into Indian cooking.

Without the invaluable help of our mother and the constant encouragement of our father, this book would not have been written. We are truly grateful for their love and support.

Flavours & Spices® wishes you: '*khav, piyo aur mouj karlow!*'
'Eat, drink and have a happy meal!'

Sereena, Alexa and Priya

'Our beautiful mum in her younger days dreaming of a Bollywood career'

The Indian spice box (*masala dabba*)

The ubiquitous Indian spice box, or *masala dabba,* seen in all Indian houses can be compared with the presence nowadays of the salt and pepper mills in every house in Europe and America. It is an essential item for anyone starting out with Indian cooking. At this stage you may be asking yourself the question – how will a spice box help me cook a good Indian meal? Here, we are going to show you how to use the spice box and gradually educate you about the spices and their uses, so that with every meal you prepare using it, your expertise will grow.

What is the Indian spice box? Essentially it has an outer container with seven to nine inner pots. Sometimes there are individual lids for each small inner pot, and sometimes a single large lid to cover all the pots at once. Lids are necessary to preserve the spice aroma. We supply a spice spoon with our ready-made spice boxes (see page 9) – however, if you do not have one then 1 spice spoon is generally equivalent to ¹/₂ teaspoon.

To make a great Indian meal, it is essential to have a stock of fresh spices. Each spice or masala, whether sold in a packet or box, will begin to lose its qualities once opened, so it is essential that you empty the contents into a spice pot or jar and close the lid after each use to maintain optimum quality.

Spice benefits

Another question you may be asking is – why do Indians use spices? Is it only to enhance flavour and to remove the raw taste of vegetables and meats, or is there another reason? Yes, there is another reason… traditionally spices were used to protect against food-borne infections. Before the invention of refrigeration, non-cooked and cooked foods would deteriorate at a fast rate, which was a serious threat to people living in hot climates. Spoilage of meat products occurs particularly fast, which is why meat recipes have a higher spice content than vegetables. Another reason could be that we 'eat to sweat', meaning that people in steamy places cool down with perspiration, so spicy food had a desirable benefit. Whatever the reasons, we are interested in evoking the spices themselves and what they have to offer in terms of flavour.

Apart from their tongue-tantalizing properties, spices are also good for health. They are known to have micronutrients as well as antioxidant effects. Some natural chemicals within spices also aid good digestion. Many people have asked us whether spices are good for pregnant women and children. We would say that during pregnancy so many changes prevail in the body that the mother-to-be must discover what is best for her. We have noted that many pregnant Indian women eat less spicy food or prefer to incorporate more yogurt in their diet, as this subdues the 'hotness' of the meal, but this may be only for a short time before she begins to enjoy spicy food again.

Young children also generally eat less spicy food. This could be due to the fact that their palates have not yet developed to appreciate all the exotic flavours available. However, there are some great mild curries in this book that are perfect for introducing young palates to the joys of Indian cooking.

The spice trade

The history of spices is so extensively woven into the trade history of the world, that it is only right that we mention its importance here. The Egyptian spice expeditions to the east coast of Africa are recorded as early as three and four thousand years ago with medicines dating back to 1550 BC. Some of these plants were not native to Egypt at that time, which means that the spice trade must have been in existence. The Egyptians used spices not only for embalming but also for flavouring foods, and in ceremonial rites where spice oils were used for anointing.

The Northern Europeans in the Middle Ages began to use spices and herbs brought back by the Crusaders who had bought 'the wealth of the Orient' from the Italians in the markets of the Mediterranean basin. With increasing demand for spices, which were sold at extortionate prices and even used as currency in the case of pepper, trade routes needed to be found. The Arabs controlled the trade routes to the East, where the Spanish and the Portuguese wanted to share the profits as well. The Age of Discovery brought Vasco Da Gama to the shores of India in 1498, breaking the monopoly of the spice trade of the Arabs. The Dutch and the British were also beneficiaries of the spice trade; with the Dutch still having a foothold up until the Second World War. Due to the extensive international trading, Indian food was influenced by the Portuguese, Arabs, Chinese, Mongols and the Hindu Emperors. All these nations contributed to what is known today as Indian cuisine, and spices are an indelible part of this.

The medicinal properties of spices are also recognized. The traditional Ayurvedic medicine of India has roots in medicinal herbs and spices and is in demand as an alternative form of medicine. Scientific studies suggest that Indian food ingredients including turmeric, cloves, ginger, aniseed, mustard, saffron, cardamom and garlic, can help prevent different types of cancers because of their antioxidant and anti-carcinogenic properties.

The spice spoon

You will notice that every recipe in this book measures spices either by a teaspoon or spice spoon. A spice spoon is a specially made spoon sold with our ready-made spice boxes. However, if you do not have one you can use the general conversion that 1 spice spoon is equivalent to $\frac{1}{2}$ teaspoon.

Planning a meal

Traditionally, the starter and the main meal are served at the same time and you choose what to eat first. These days, a variation of the main dish with a dip is served as a starter and is popular with a drink prior to dinner.

Usually, a meal consists of a main dish, a dal, one or two vegetable dishes and a raita or chutney. The dessert is usually a dish consisting of fruit. Plan an Indian meal by first selecting the main dish. If this is spicy then choose the other side dishes to complement it. For example, Yogurt-marinated Lamb (page 62) has spices that are very mild. To complement this, you may like to serve Kashmiri Potatoes (page 102) and Mango or Coriander Chutney (pages 144 and 145). A raita would not be necessary in this case. If the main dish is rich and spicy, choose a raita and a mild vegetable dish.

When preparing for a party, multiply the amount of ingredients according to your number of guests. Include a lentil dish in case the meal requires a sauce. Every meal is served with rice as well as a flatbread like Chapati, Naan (see pages 138 and 139).

Making a ginger–garlic paste

100 g (3½ oz) garlic cloves, peeled
100 g (3½ oz) ginger, chopped
1–2 teaspoons oil

Blitz all the ingredients in a blender to a smooth paste, adding more oil if necessary. Pour into an airtight container and store in the fridge for up to 4 weeks.

Use 2 teaspoons in a recipe that serves 4 people. To store in the freezer, place 2 teaspoon quantities into ice cube tray compartments and freeze until required.

Essential preparation tips

Storing fresh coriander

Buy fresh coriander, which is medium-green in colour, tender and aromatic, as this will ensure optimum flavour.
To store:
- cut the ends of the stems;
- put the whole bunch in a jar with water as you would with flowers;
- cover the leaves with a plastic bag and place in the fridge, changing the water every two days;
- remove any wilted leaves and return the bunch to the fridge.

Another method of storing fresh coriander is to chop the leaves and stems (these are equally nutritious and full of flavour) finely. Place them in an ice cube tray, cover with water and freeze until required.

Making paneer cheese

Paneer is readily available in most supermarkets but if you do have time, it's easy to make your own. Just follow the recipe below, which makes approximately 200–250 g (7–8 oz) paneer.

2 litres (3½ pints) whole milk
Juice of 2 lemons, strained

Line a colander with muslin or a thin cotton cloth. Bring the milk to the boil in a heavy saucepan over a medium–high heat. When the milk is fully boiled, reduce the heat, stirring occasionally, to prevent sticking to the bottom of the saucepan.

Pour the lemon juice on to the surface of the milk in a steady stream and stir continuously. Stir gently when the milk begins to show signs of curdling and clumping at the surface. You should have a large white mass of curdled milk (the paneer) on top of a yellow-green liquid (the whey). If not, then add some more lemon juice and gently stir.

Strain into the muslin-lined colander and discard the whey. Tie the ends of the muslin loosely above the paneer. Run it under cold water for a few minutes and then, wearing rubber gloves, squeeze tightly to remove any remaining whey and form into a ball. Hang the paneer by the top ends of the muslin cloth for an hour to drain as much of the whey as possible. Remove the paneer from the cloth and place on a board, cutting to the desired size before using.

Peeling and crushing/chopping garlic

There are two ways to peel a clove of garlic:
• dip the cloves in water for 10 minutes before peeling, this will make the peel come away easily.
• press a clove under the flat side of a chef's knife. The skin will split, making it easier to peel away.
Chopping the garlic using a little water will make it less sticky and easier to handle.

Peeling fresh tomatoes

Drop whole tomatoes into boiling water for a few minutes, rinse with cold water and peel away the skins.

Cutting fresh green chillies

Apply a little cooking oil to the knife blade and the tips of your fingers when cutting or deseeding chillies. This will prevent any irritation and spray, which can occur when handling chillies. Always wash your hands thoroughly after preparing chillies.

Useful ingredients

For your larder:	For your fridge/freezer:
basmati rice	butter
plain flour	coconut milk
wholewheat (atta) flour	eggs
gram flour	natural yogurt
salt	Greek yogurt
black pepper	fresh coriander
sodium bicarbonate	chicken fillets
sugar	diced lamb
chickpeas	lamb mince
red kidney beans	mixed frozen vegetables
mung dal beans	
red split lentils	
tomato purée	**For your vegetable basket:**
tinned chopped plum	tomatoes
tomatoes	lemons
dried mint	limes
ground nutmeg	potatoes
ground cinnamon	garlic
stock cubes	chillies
oil (we favour rapeseed oil,	ginger
but any oil can be used)	onions
	shallots

Masala Dabba — The Spice Box

This Indian spice box will be your right-hand tool when creating the recipes in this book or any kind of Indian cooking. Use the list of spices below to create your very own *masala dabba* or buy a ready-made Flavours & Spices one that holds all of the 13 spices you need to cook any of the recipes in this book.

Chilli (*Capsicum family*)
Chillies vary in colour, shape, heat levels and pungency from variety to variety. They are a rich source of vitamin C. Whole chillies are dried and then crushed to give ground chilli.

Coriander (*Coriandrum sativum*)
All the parts of the coriander plant are used in Indian cooking; the seeds are ground and used to thicken and flavour dishes and the fresh green leaves are used in garnishes.

Cumin seeds (*Cuminum cyminum*)
Cumin seeds are strongly aromatic and the aroma varies according to whether the spice is fried or dry roasted. It stimulates the appetite and acts as a digestive.

Ground cumin (*Cuminum cyminum*)
Ground cumin gives a slightly bitter and sweet taste at the same time. It is used as a seasoning for lime- or chilli-based sauces.

Fennel (*Foeniculum vulgare*)
This is a sweet and aromatic spice with an aniseed-type flavour. Fennel seeds contain important antioxidants, with anti-cancerous properties.

Ginger (*Zingiber officinale*)
Fresh or dry ginger is aromatic, pungent and hot. It can be used in sweet and savoury dishes. It is known to help digestion and calm mental activity.

In addition to the 13 spices below, some recipes in this book may also call for a few other spices. Therefore, it may be useful to also keep a supply of the following spices and herbs: nutmeg, saffron, fresh or dried curry leaves, ground cinnamon, asafoetida, whole black peppercorns and star anise.

Turmeric (*Curcuma longa*)
The root of this plant looks very similar to ginger but the flesh is a deep orange colour. When dried and ground, turmeric gives a beautiful yellow colour to any food cooked with it.

Cinnamon (*Cinnamomum zeylanicum*)
Cinnamon sticks are carved from the bark of the cinnamon tree. Cinnamon has a sweet taste and a fragrant aroma.
Bay leaf (*Cinnamomum cassia*)
The Indian bay leaf is aromatic and bitter in flavour. These leaves are used whole to flavour mainly meat dishes.

Cardamom (*Elettaria cardamomum*)
Cardamom has a sweet, spicy and pungent flavour. The green variety is used in both savoury and sweet dishes.

Cloves (*Syzygium aromaticum*)
Cloves are strongly pungent and sweet. Very small quantities are required to flavour dishes. Clove oil is used topically as it has antiseptic and anti-inflammatory properties.

Mustard seeds (*Brassica nigra*)
In Indian cooking, the whole seeds are fried quickly in oil to give a hot and spicy flavour once the seeds have popped.

Garam masala
A blend of several strongly aromatic spices designed to add flavour, fragrance and heat to many Indian dishes.

Halp-aahaar

Little Snacks and Starters

Aam Aur Saeb Ka Shorba

Mango and Apple Soup

1 tablespoon butter

2 garlic cloves, crushed

2 cm (¾ inch) piece of ginger, grated

1 onion, finely chopped

1 mango (not too ripe), stoned, peeled and chopped

2 eating apples, peeled, cored and chopped

1 green chilli, deseeded and chopped

200 ml (7 fl oz) coconut milk

400 ml (14 fl oz) natural yogurt

2 teaspoons lemon juice

Salt and freshly ground black pepper

To finish

Fresh mint leaves, finely chopped

SERVES 6

FROM YOUR SPICE BOX

WHOLE SPICES

½ teaspoon (1 spice spoon) cumin seeds

Heat the butter in a heavy-based saucepan over a medium heat and add the cumin seeds, garlic and ginger. Fry for 30 seconds and then add the onion, frying until the onion is lightly browned.

Set aside 2 tablespoons of the chopped mango to use as a finishing garnish. Add the remaining mango, apple, chilli, salt and pepper to the cumin and onions and cook for 2 minutes over a medium heat.

Remove from the heat and transfer to a food processor or blender. Blitz until smooth and strain to remove the fibres from the mango if you prefer an ultra smooth consistency.

Return to the saucepan over a medium heat. Add 500 ml (17 fl oz) water, bring to the boil and continue to stir for 5 minutes.

Whisk the coconut milk and yogurt together in a separate bowl and add this to the saucepan. Bring the soup back to simmering point, mix in the lemon juice and finish with the reserved chopped mango and finely chopped mint leaves before serving.

Note: this soup is also delicious served chilled as a summer fruit soup.

Our Aunt had a mango tree in her garden; when in fruit it kept her busy with mango chutneys, desserts and soups. This delicious golden soup reminds us of seeing her in the kitchen with a mound of mangoes waiting to be transformed.

Gajar Aur Naryal Dood Ka Shorba

Carrot and Coconut Soup

1 tablespoon butter

½ tablespoon oil

1 large onion, roughly chopped

2 cm (¾ inch) piece of ginger, grated

250 g (8 oz) carrots, chopped

1 green chilli, deseeded and chopped

2 curry leaves (optional)

300 ml (½ pint) coconut milk

2 teaspoons lemon juice

1 tablespoon finely chopped fresh coriander leaves and stalks

Salt and ground black pepper

SERVES 4

FROM YOUR SPICE BOX

WHOLE SPICES

½ teaspoon (1 spice spoon) cumin seeds

½ teaspoon (1 spice spoon) mustard seeds

1 bay leaf

To finish

Natural yogurt (whisked smooth)

Fresh coriander leaves

Heat the butter and oil in a heavy-based saucepan over a medium heat and add the whole spices.

When the seeds begin to sizzle, add the onion, ginger, carrots, green chilli, curry leaves (if using), salt and pepper. Fry for a few minutes until the onions are lightly browned.

Add 1 litre (1¾ pints) water, cover and cook for 30–35 minutes, or until the carrots are soft.

Remove the bay leaf and curry leaves (if using) and blitz the mixture in a food processor or blender to a smooth purée.

Whisk the coconut milk in a separate bowl to make it smooth. Return the puréed soup to the saucepan over a medium heat and add the whisked coconut milk, lemon juice and fresh coriander. Bring to the boil and check the seasoning.

Serve finished with a swirl of yogurt and some fresh coriander leaves. It can be served with fresh, crusty bread or Naan bread (page 138).

Sitafal Ka Shorba

Spicy Butternut Squash Soup

3 tablespoons yellow split
  chickpeas (channa dal)
2 tablespoons butter
2 onions, finely chopped
2 cm (¾ inch) piece of ginger,
  grated
2 garlic cloves, crushed
200 g (7 oz) butternut squash,
  peeled and roughly chopped
100 g (3½ oz) baby plum
  tomatoes, cut in half
2 teaspoons lemon juice
Salt and freshly ground black
  pepper

To finish
Natural yogurt (whisked
  smooth)

SERVES 4–6

FROM YOUR SPICE BOX
WHOLE SPICES
¼ teaspoon (½ spice spoon)
  mustard seeds
½ teaspoon (1 spice spoon)
  cumin seeds

GROUND SPICES
¼ teaspoon (½ spice spoon)
  ginger
¼ teaspoon (½ spice spoon)
  turmeric
¼ teaspoon (½ spice spoon)
  chilli

Soak the yellow split chickpeas (channa dal) in hot water for a few hours or overnight. Drain from their soaking water when ready to use.

Heat the butter in a large saucepan over a medium heat and add the whole spices. When the mustard and cumin seeds begin to sizzle add the onions, ginger and garlic and fry until lightly browned.

Add the butternut squash, drained split chickpeas, tomatoes and ground spices. Cook for 5 minutes stirring occasionally.

Add 750 ml (1¼ pints) water and bring it to the boil. Reduce the heat and leave to simmer for 20–25 minutes, or until the butternut squash and split chickpeas are soft.

Transfer the soup to a food processor or blender and blitz until smooth. Return the soup to the saucepan over a medium heat, mix in the lemon juice and check the seasoning. Serve finished with a swirl of yogurt.

Our mother would rush out to the garden when an unexpected guest arrived, gather the ingredients she needed and make up a quick batch of this wonderful soup.

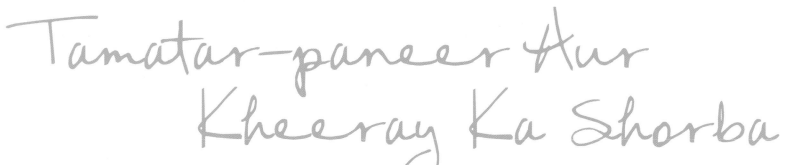

Tamatar-paneer Aur Kheeray Ka Shorba

Tomato, Cheese and Cucumber Soup

500 g (1 lb) ripe tomatoes

2 tablespoons butter

1 onion, finely chopped

2 cm (¾ inch) piece of ginger, grated

2 garlic cloves, crushed

1 small potato, finely chopped

1 teaspoon Demerara sugar

100 g (3½ oz) paneer, either home-made (see page 11) or shop-bought, diced into very small cubes (plus extra, to finish)

1 teaspoon lemon juice

Salt and freshly ground black pepper

SERVES 4

FROM YOUR SPICE BOX

WHOLE SPICES

½ teaspoon (1 spice spoon) cumin seeds

GROUND SPICES

½ teaspoon (1 spice spoon) coriander

To finish

Fresh coriander leaves, finely chopped

Cucumber, diced into very small cubes

Plunge the tomatoes into boiling water for 5 minutes. Run them under cold water to cool down and then peel away the skin and chop roughly.

Heat the butter in a heavy-based saucepan over a medium heat and add the whole spice, followed by the onion, ginger, garlic, potato, tomatoes, sugar, ground spice and salt and pepper.

Fry for 4–5 minutes then add 450 ml (¾ pint) water. Cover and simmer for 15 minutes or until the potato is soft.

Transfer to a food processor or blender and blitz to a smooth purée. When cool, return to the saucepan over a medium heat, add more water if it is looking too thick and bring back to the boil.

Add the diced paneer and lemon juice and cook over a medium heat for 1–3 minutes.

Finish with fresh coriander, very small cubes of cucumber and a little diced paneer.

Pakoras

Vegetable Fritters

Oil, for deep frying

For the batter
125 g (4 oz) gram flour
$^1/_2$ teaspoon bicarbonate of
    soda
2 tablespoons finely chopped
    fresh coriander
2 garlic cloves, finely crushed
1 tablespoon lemon juice
Salt and freshly ground black
    pepper

For the filling
2 potatoes, cut into 2–3 mm
    ($^1/_8$ inch) slices
2 cauliflower or broccoli
    florets, thinly sliced
1 onion, sliced into rings
15 green beans, trimmed and
    cut in half
1 small green pepper, deseeded
    and sliced into rings

SERVES 6

FROM YOUR SPICE BOX
WHOLE SPICES
$^1/_2$ teaspoon (1 spice spoon)
    cumin seeds

GROUND SPICES
1 teaspoon (2 spice spoons)
    chilli
$^1/_2$ teaspoon (1 spice spoon)
    coriander
$^1/_2$ teaspoon (1 spice spoon)
    ginger
$^1/_2$ teaspoon (1 spice spoon)
    turmeric

Heat a small frying pan over a medium heat and dry roast the cumin seeds for 30 seconds until the seeds turn dark brown. When cool, coarsely grind the toasted cumin seeds using a pestle and mortar and tip them into a mixing bowl.

To make the batter, sift the flour into a bowl with the bicarbonate of soda, salt and the toasted ground cumin. Add some black pepper, the ground spices, fresh coriander, garlic and lemon juice.

Slowly add 150 ml ($^1/_4$ pint) water and stir with a spatula to form a smooth and thick batter. Use more water or flour if necessary to achieve the required consistency of batter, which should be thick enough to coat the vegetables. Alternatively, use a hand blender and blend until smooth. Set aside.

Heat the oil in a saucepan until a drop of the batter fried in the oil rises quickly and sizzles (alternatively, use a deep fryer at 180°C/350°F). Dip a few vegetables into the batter and then place them slowly into the hot oil. Turn the vegetables over a few times so that they are evenly browned.

Remove with a slotted spoon and drain on kitchen paper. Fry the rest of the vegetables in batches.

Delicious served hot with Spicy Tomato Dip (page 148) and Mint and Yogurt Chutney (page 152).

We have fond memories of sitting over a cup of tea on a still afternoon in Kashmir; and Mum coming to us with a plate of sizzling hot pakoras. This kept us totally entertained guessing which vegetable was hidden in the batter – the aim being to save ourselves from the chilli pakora!

Samosa

Vegetable-stuffed Pastry

For the pastry

150 g (5 oz) plain flour

½ teaspoon salt

40 g (1½ oz) unsalted butter or ghee

60 ml (2½ fl oz) warm water

For the filling

2 tablespoons unsalted butter or ghee

1 large onion, finely sliced

3 garlic cloves, crushed

2 cm (¾ inch) ginger, grated

250 g (8 oz) potatoes, cut into 2 cm (¾ inch) cubes

50 g (2 oz) frozen peas

1 teaspoon lemon juice

4 tablespoons finely chopped fresh coriander

Salt and ground black pepper

Oil, for deep frying

SERVES 6–8

FROM YOUR SPICE BOX

WHOLE SPICES

½ teaspoon (1 spice spoon) cumin seeds

GROUND SPICES

1 teaspoon (2 spice spoons) chilli

½ teaspoon (1 spice spoon) coriander

½ teaspoon (1 spice spoon) cumin

¾ teaspoon (1½ spice spoons) garam masala

½ teaspoon (1 spice spoon) turmeric

To make the pastry, sift the flour and salt in a bowl and add the whole spice. Rub the butter or ghee into the flour with your fingertips until it resembles fine breadcrumbs. Slowly pour in the measured water and combine to form a single dough ball. Knead for 5 minutes on a lightly floured surface then cover and leave to rest for 1 hour at room temperature.

To make the filling, heat the butter in a heavy-based shallow pan over a medium heat and sauté the onion until light brown. Add the garlic, ginger, potatoes, ground spices, salt and pepper and fry for 5 minutes before adding the peas and lemon juice. Cover and cook, stirring, for 5 minutes or until the potato mixture turns fairly soft. Mix in the fresh coriander. Cool the mixture and divide into 18 equal portions.

Knead the rested dough for 5 minutes and divide into 9 equal balls. Cover the dough balls with a damp cloth. Roll out one dough ball on a floured surface to about 15 cm (6 inches) diameter and cut in half.

Take one half of the circle and moisten the straight edge with water then fold into a cone shape overlapping the moistened straight edge by 5 mm (¼ inch). Press to seal well.

Open the mouth of the cone and insert one portion of the filling. Seal the samosa mouth by moistening and pressing the edges together firmly. Make the second samosa from the other half-circle in the same manner and place on a lightly floured tray. Repeat, using the rest of the dough and filling.

Heat the oil in a saucepan until a drop of the batter fried in the oil rises quickly and sizzles (alternatively, use a deep fryer at 180°C/350°F). Fry the samosas in batches of 3 at a time until light brown on both sides. Remove with a slotted spoon and drain on kitchen paper.

Note: samosas can be individually frozen for up to one month before the frying stage. Just layer with baking paper in between each samosa.

A wonderful tea-time snack that we all adore!

Aloo Tikki

Potato Cakes

3 potatoes
½ onion, finely chopped
2 slices white bread, blitzed to
  breadcrumbs
1 tablespoon lemon juice
½ teaspoon freshly ground
  black pepper
1 tablespoon butter
3 tablespoons finely chopped
  fresh coriander
Oil, for shallow frying

SERVES 4–6

FROM YOUR SPICE BOX
WHOLE SPICES
½ teaspoon (1 spice spoon)
  cumin seeds
½ teaspoon (1 spice spoon)
  coriander seeds

GROUND SPICES
½ teaspoon (1 spice spoon)
  ginger
½ teaspoon (1 spice spoon)
  chilli
½ teaspoon (1 spice spoon)
  garam masala

To finish
Red onion, finely sliced
Fresh coriander leaves, finely
  chopped

Boil the potatoes in their skins until soft. Run under cold water and peel away the skin. Leave in the fridge for 15 minutes.

Heat a small frying pan over a medium heat and dry roast the cumin and coriander seeds for 30 seconds until the seeds turn dark brown. When cool, coarsely grind the toasted seeds using a pestle and mortar.

In a bowl mash the cold potatoes and then add all the other ingredients and the ground spices. Mix well until smooth. Divide into 10–12 equal portions and leave to one side.

Oil your hands and take one portion of the potato mixture and shape into a ball. Flatten each ball into a 6 cm (2¼ inch) circle.

Heat the oil on a flat griddle or frying pan over a low–medium heat. Fry each potato cake for 3–4 minutes until golden and crispy, turning once. Finish with finely sliced red onion and freshly chopped coriander.

Serve hot with Sweet and Sour Mango Chutney (page 144) or Mint and Yogurt Chutney (page 152).

We could never say no to this snack, which is also a popular street food in India.

Kheema Kababs

Lamb Kebabs

500 g (1 lb) lamb mince

1 large onion, finely chopped

4 large garlic cloves, finely chopped

2 cm (³/₄ inch) piece of ginger, finely chopped

3 tablespoons finely chopped fresh coriander

2 green chillies, deseeded and finely sliced

1 egg yolk

1 teaspoon salt

¹/₂ teaspoon freshly ground black pepper

2 teaspoons lemon juice

¹/₂ teaspoon ground cinnamon

Large pinch of ground nutmeg

¹/₂ tablespoon oil

1 teaspoon dried mint leaves or 1 tablespoon chopped fresh mint leaves

4 tablespoons gram flour

10 metal skewers or wooden bamboo sticks soaked in cold water for 30 minutes

SERVES 4–6

FROM YOUR SPICE BOX

WHOLE SPICES

2 cardamom pods, seeds finely crushed

³/₄ teaspoon (1¹/₂ spice spoons) cumin seeds

GROUND SPICES

¹/₂ teaspoon (1 spice spoon) chilli

¹/₂ teaspoon (1 spice spoon) coriander

¹/₂ teaspoon (1 spice spoon) garam masala

Spread the lamb mince in a large bowl and add all the ingredients and spices except the gram flour and cumin seeds.

Heat a griddle or frying pan over a medium heat and dry roast the gram flour for 1 minute or until light brown. Remove from the heat and add to the mince.

Return the griddle or frying pan to a medium heat until hot and dry roast the cumin seeds for 30 seconds. When cool, grind the seeds using a pestle and mortar before adding to the mince.

Knead the mince mixture for 2–3 minutes, then cover and refrigerate overnight. Divide the mince into 10 equal balls. With wet hands, wrap the mince evenly around each skewer into a long sausage shape of around 15 cm (6 inches).

Cover a grill rack with foil and make a few holes in the foil at various places for the excess oil to drain off. Place the kebabs on the foil and cook under a preheated grill over a medium heat for 10–15 minutes on each side.

This is great served hot with Coriander Chutney (page 145). It can also be made into burgers and served in fresh bread rolls.

Alexa remembers helping Mum roll out these kebabs in anticipation that she could eat them quicker – the trick always worked!

Bhindi Churma

Crispy Okra Chips

200 g (7 oz) okra
2 tablespoons lemon juice
1 tablespoon white rice flour
3 tablespoons gram flour
Salt
Oil, for deep frying

SERVES 4

FROM YOUR SPICE BOX
GROUND SPICES
½ teaspoon (1 spice spoon) ginger
½ teaspoon (1 spice spoon) chilli
1 teaspoon (2 spice spoons) coriander

Wash the okra and dry each piece well using a clean kitchen tea towel. Top, but don't 'tail' the okras and slice each one lengthways.

In a large bowl mix the ground spices, salt and lemon juice with the okra. Use your hands to mix but make sure you wash your hands thoroughly after mixing.

In a separate bowl mix the rice flour and gram flour with 4 tablespoons water to a smooth paste and pour over the okra, mixing well to coat but taking care not to break the okra.

Heat the oil in a khadi or wok over a medium heat. When the oil is hot, fry the okra in batches for a few minutes until golden brown. Remove with a slotted spoon and drain on sheets of kitchen paper.

Serve hot with Coriander Chutney (page 145).

These crispy okra chips are the perfect party snack.

Macchli Tikki

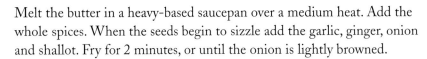

Indian-spiced Fish Cakes

1½ tablespoons butter

3 garlic cloves, crushed

1 cm (½ inch) piece of ginger, grated

1 onion, finely chopped

1 shallot, finely chopped

2 potatoes, cooked

400 g (13 oz) white fish fillets, such as haddock or cod, skinned

4–5 tablespoons finely chopped fresh coriander

2 eggs, beaten

125 g (4 oz) fresh white breadcrumbs

Salt

Oil, for shallow frying

SERVES 4

FROM YOUR SPICE BOX

WHOLE SPICES

½ teaspoon (1 spice spoon) cumin seeds

¼ teaspoon (½ spice spoon) mustard seeds

GROUND SPICES

½ teaspoon (1 spice spoon) chilli

½ teaspoon (1 spice spoon) garam masala

¼ teaspoon (½ spice spoon) cumin

½ teaspoon (1 spice spoon) ginger

1 teaspoon (2 spice spoons) coriander

½ teaspoon (1 spice spoon) turmeric

Melt the butter in a heavy-based saucepan over a medium heat. Add the whole spices. When the seeds begin to sizzle add the garlic, ginger, onion and shallot. Fry for 2 minutes, or until the onion is lightly browned.

Remove from the heat momentarily and add the ground spices, except the turmeric. Leave to cool.

Once cool, transfer the mixture to a food processor or blender and blitz to a thick mixture.

Mash the potatoes in a separate bowl and set aside.

Poach the fish pieces in water with a little salt and the turmeric from the ground spices for 5–8 minutes. Drain then wash away the turmeric. Dry the fish pieces gently with kitchen paper. Flake the fish and discard any bones. Add the fish to the bowl with the mashed potatoes, mash and mix well. Add the onion mixture and fresh coriander and combine.

Take a portion of the fish mixture and shape into a patty about 6 cm (2½ inches) wide. Lightly coat the patty with the beaten egg and then dip into the breadcrumbs, covering both sides.

Shallow fry over a medium heat for 3–4 minutes on each side until crisp and golden, turning once.

Serve with Apple, Ginger and Cinnamon Chutney (page 147) and lemon wedges.

Our children just wouldn't eat fish until we turned it into these fish cakes – perfect for little hands to grab hold of.

Aloo Aur Anaar Ka Chaat

Potato with Pomegranate

4 potatoes

2 tablespoons chopped fresh
   coriander

½ green chilli, deseeded and
   finely chopped

½ small red onion, finely
   chopped

1 teaspoon lemon juice

2 tablespoons pomegranate
   seeds

Salt

To finish

6 tablespoons natural yogurt
   (whisked smooth), to finish

SERVES 4

FROM YOUR SPICE BOX

WHOLE SPICES

¼ teaspoon (½ spice spoon)
   cumin seeds

Boil the potatoes in their skins until soft. Run under cold water, peel and leave to cool completely.

Heat a small frying pan over a medium heat and dry roast the cumin seeds for 30 seconds until the seeds turn dark brown. When cool, grind the toasted seeds using a pestle and mortar to a fine powder.

Cut the cooled potatoes into small cubes and place in a bowl with the remaining ingredients and ground cumin seeds. Mix well.

Put the yogurt in a separate serving bowl to be added as a dressing.

Serve as a starter or tea-time snack with Tamarind Chutney (page 153).

Chaat is instantly refreshing on a steamy, hot day.

Paneer Bhujia

Scrambled Paneer

3 tablespoons oil

2–3 fresh or dried curry leaves
(optional)

2 small garlic cloves, crushed

1 cm (½ inch) piece of ginger,
grated

1 small green chilli, deseeded
and finely chopped

1 small onion, chopped

1 small potato, finely chopped

250 g (8 oz) paneer, either
home-made (see page 11)
or shop-bought, crumbled

3 cherry tomatoes, finely
chopped

3 tablespoons finely chopped
fresh coriander

Salt and freshly ground black
pepper

SERVES 4

FROM YOUR SPICE BOX

WHOLE SPICES

½ teaspoon (1 spice spoon)
cumin seeds

¼ teaspoon (½ spice spoon)
mustard seeds

GROUND SPICES

¼ teaspoon (½ spice spoon)
ginger

½ teaspoon (1 spice spoon)
turmeric

½ teaspoon (1 spice spoon)
coriander

½ teaspoon (1 spice spoon)
chilli

Heat the oil in a frying pan over a medium heat. When hot add the whole spices and curry leaves (if using).

When the spices begin to sizzle add the garlic, ginger and chilli and mix well. Then add the onion and potato and fry for 2–3 minutes. Add the crumbled paneer and fry for 1 minute. Mix in the tomatoes and fry for a further 1–2 minutes.

Remove from the heat temporarily and mix in the ground spices. Cook for 5 minutes over a medium heat.

Add 200 ml (7 fl oz) water, stir, cover and cook over a low heat for 10–15 minutes, or until the potatoes are soft and some liquid still remains. Mix in the coriander and check the seasoning.

Serve with Chapatis (page 139) or Basmati Rice (page 120) as a main dish. Alternatively, serve with fresh, crusty bread for breakfast or a light snack.

This is the fastest breakfast or light lunch our Mum could ever put together – she had the paneer draining while frying the onions and tomatoes on the stove. The result, as usual, is gastronomical!

Tamatar Aur Pyaz Ka Omelette

Indian Tomato and Onion Omelette

6 eggs

1 small green chilli, deseeded and finely chopped

1 tablespoon finely chopped fresh coriander

1 tablespoon milk

2 tablespoons oil

1 small onion, finely chopped

1 tomato, finely chopped

Salt and freshly ground black pepper

SERVES 2

FROM YOUR SPICE BOX

WHOLE SPICES

¼ teaspoon (½ spice spoon) cumin seeds

GROUND SPICES

A good pinch of chilli

Whisk the eggs with the ground spice, green chilli, fresh coriander, milk and seasoning.

Heat the oil in a frying pan over a medium heat. When the oil is hot add the whole spice. When the cumin seeds begin to sizzle add the onion and fry until lightly browned. Add the tomato and fry for a further 1–2 minutes.

Reduce the heat to low and pour in the egg mixture. Wait until the mixture bubbles at the side, then push the mixture to the middle of the frying pan letting the liquid slide into the sides of the frying pan.

Cook until the omelette is light and fluffy, or until it has come away from the side of the pan. Gently fold one-third of the omelette into the middle and bring the other side to meet it. Cut in two and flip over.

This is great served immediately as a brunch or lunch dish with Deep-fried Bread (page 140) and tomato wedges.

Namkeen Chawal Ka Chilla

Savoury Rice Flour Pancakes

200 g (7 oz) white rice flour
½ teaspoon salt
Oil, for frying

SERVES 4

Note: rice flour will swell
and thicken if not used
straight away. If the batter
is left to sit for more than
10 minutes you may need
to mix in a little water to
thin it out.

FROM YOUR SPICE BOX
WHOLE SPICES
½ teaspoon (1 spice spoon)
  cumin seeds

GROUND SPICES
¼ teaspoon (½ spice spoon)
  chilli

In a bowl mix together the rice flour, salt and whole spices with
260 ml (8½ fl oz) of water to make a smooth, thin batter.

Heat a flat griddle or frying pan with a little oil over a medium heat.
When the pan is hot use a ladle to pour the pancake mixture on to the
griddle to form a circle of about 15–17 cm (6–7 inches). When the
pancake starts to crisp at the edges, flip the pancake over and cook until
golden brown.

Serve the pancakes with Tomato Salad (page 37) and chunky fresh lime
wedges. See photo opposite.

*The crispier and thinner the better – what a change from
regular flour crepes.*

Meetha Chawal Ka Chilla

Sweet Rice Flour Pancakes

200 g (7 oz) white rice flour
40 g (1½ oz) caster sugar
Oil, for frying
Sifted icing sugar, for dusting

SERVES 4

In a bowl mix together the rice flour and sugar with 260 ml (8½ fl oz)
water to make a smooth batter.

Heat a flat griddle or frying pan with a little oil over a medium heat. When
the pan is hot use a ladle to pour the pancake mixture on to the griddle to
form a circle of about 10–12 cm (4–5 inches). When the pancake starts to
crisp at the edges, flip the pancake over and cook until golden brown. Serve
with Honey, Yogurt and Cinnamon Ice Cream (page 168).

Mung Ankur Salad

Sprouted Bean Salad

400 g (13 oz) beansprouts

1 green pepper, finely chopped

1 small onion, finely chopped

2 garlic cloves, crushed

2 tablespoons finely chopped
  fresh coriander

1 green chilli, deseeded and
  finely sliced

2 tablespoons lemon juice

1 tablespoon olive oil

Salt and freshly ground black
  pepper

To finish

1 plum tomato, sliced

SERVES 6

FROM YOUR SPICE BOX

WHOLE SPICES

½ teaspoon (1 spice spoon)
  mustard seeds

GROUND SPICES

¼ teaspoon (½ spice spoon)
  chilli

½ teaspoon (1 spice spoon)
  cumin

1 teaspoon (2 spice spoons)
  turmeric

Tip all the ingredients into a large salad bowl except the olive oil and the whole and ground spices.

Heat the olive oil in a small frying pan over a medium heat and add the whole spice. When the mustard seeds begin to pop, remove from the heat and mix the ground spices into the oil in the pan.

Pour the spiced oil over the salad. Toss the salad until the yellow colour of the spice comes through.

Finish with tomato slices and serve as a starter or as an accompaniment to a light lunch.

Mum insisted that we eat a bean salad once in a while because it's so healthy, as well as refreshing.

Tamatar Kuchumber
Tomato Salad

500 g (1 lb) plum tomatoes on the vine, deseeded and finely chopped

1 small red onion, finely chopped

2 tablespoons finely chopped fresh coriander

1 tablespoon finely chopped fresh mint leaves

1 green chilli, deseeded and finely sliced

2 garlic cloves, crushed

1 tablespoon olive oil

Juice of 1 lime

Salt and freshly ground black pepper

SERVES 4

FROM YOUR SPICE BOX

WHOLE SPICES

¼ teaspoon (½ spice spoon) cumin seeds

¼ teaspoon (½ spice spoon) mustard seeds

Heat a small frying pan over a medium heat and dry roast the cumin seeds for 30 seconds until the seeds turn dark brown. When cool, coarsely grind the cumin seeds using a pestle and mortar and set aside.

Place the tomatoes, onion, fresh coriander, fresh mint leaves, green chilli, garlic, seasoning and dry-roasted cumin seeds all together in a bowl.

Heat the oil in a small frying pan and add the mustard seeds. Fry until the seeds begin to pop and then pour the seeds and oil over the tomato salad mixture. Gently combine the ingredients.

Squeeze the lime juice over the salad, cover and leave at room temperature for 25 minutes to allow the flavours to develop.

Serve chilled as a starter or an accompaniment to a main dish.

Murgh

Chicken

Murgh Aur Palak

Chicken with Spinach

500 g (1 lb) baby spinach leaves

3 tablespoons oil

500 g (1 lb) skinless chicken breast fillets, cut into bite-sized pieces

3 tablespoons tomato purée

Salt

SERVES 4

FROM YOUR SPICE BOX

WHOLE SPICES

¼ teaspoon (½ spice spoon) cumin seeds

GROUND SPICES

1 teaspoon (2 spice spoons) ginger

1 teaspoon (2 spice spoons) coriander

1 teaspoon (2 spice spoons) fennel

¼ teaspoon (½ spice spoon) cumin

1 teaspoon (2 spice spoons) chilli

½ teaspoon (1 spice spoon) garam masala

Wash the spinach and leave to drain until all the water has gone.

Heat 1 tablespoon of the oil in a saucepan over a medium heat and add the spinach leaves with ½ teaspoon salt.

Stir and cook for 3–4 minutes, breaking down the spinach leaves with the back of a wooden spoon till a pulp is formed, but still some liquid remains. Leave to one side.

Heat the remaining oil in a heavy-based saucepan over a medium heat and add the whole spice. When the seeds begin to sizzle add the chicken and some more salt.

Cover and cook, stirring occasionally, for 10 minutes until the chicken pieces are golden brown.

Temporarily remove from the heat and add the ground spices. Return to the heat, mix in the tomato purée and fry for 1 minute before adding 300 ml (½ pint) water.

Cover and cook for 10 minutes or until the chicken is tender. Add the spinach with its liquid and cook for a further 5 minutes.

Serve with Crispy Okra Chips (page 28) and Saffron Rice (page 122).

Bhuna Murgh

Spiced Pan-fried Chicken

3 tablespoons oil

500 g (1 lb) skinless chicken breast fillets, cut into bite-sized pieces

2 tablespoons natural yogurt (whisked smooth)

Salt and freshly ground black pepper

Finely chopped fresh coriander, to finish

SERVES 4

FROM YOUR SPICE BOX

WHOLE SPICES

¼ teaspoon (½ spice spoon) cumin seeds

2 bay leaves

1 cinnamon stick

2 cardamom pods, crushed

1 clove, ground

GROUND SPICES

1 teaspoon (2 spice spoons) chilli

½ teaspoon (1 spice spoon) ginger

½ teaspoon (1 spice spoon) garam masala

¼ teaspoon (½ spice spoon) cumin

Heat the oil in a heavy-based frying pan over a medium heat and add the whole spices. Fry for 30 seconds then add the chicken, salt, pepper and 200 ml (7 fl oz) water.

Reduce the heat to low, cover and cook, stirring occasionally for 5–8 minutes, or until the oil separates from the water.

Then lift off the lid and cook until the water evaporates. Continue to cook in the dry pan until the chicken is golden brown. Mix in the yogurt and fry until no liquid remains.

Remove from the heat momentarily, add the ground spices and 2 tablespoons water, return to the heat and fry for 1 minute. Keep the chicken moist by adding more water if needed.

Top with chopped coriander before serving.

Serve with Sautéed Mushrooms (page 108), Saffron Rice (page 122) and/or Naan bread (page 138).

This quick and easy recipe makes a wonderful supper.

Makhani Murgh

Butter Chicken

100 ml (3½ fl oz) natural
  yogurt
40 g (1½ oz) ground almonds
200 g (7 oz) tomatoes, peeled
  and chopped
1 tablespoon tomato purée
2 cm (¾ inch) piece of ginger
2 garlic cloves
1 teaspoon ground cinnamon
1 green chilli, deseeded and
  cut in half lengthways
500 g (1 lb) skinless chicken
  breast fillets, cut into bite-
  sized pieces
60 g (2½ oz) ghee or 50 g
  (2 oz) unsalted butter and
  1 tablespoon oil
1 onion, finely sliced
150–200 ml (5–7 fl oz) milk
2 tablespoons single cream
2 tablespoons finely chopped
  fresh coriander
Salt and freshly ground black
  pepper

SERVES 4

FROM YOUR SPICE BOX

WHOLE SPICES

2 cardamom pods, crushed
2 cloves
2 bay leaves

GROUND SPICES

½ teaspoon (1 spice spoon)
  chilli
½ teaspoon (1 spice spoon)
  fennel
½ teaspoon (1 spice spoon)
  garam masala

Put the yogurt, ground almonds, tomatoes, tomato purée, ginger, garlic, cinnamon, green chilli, seasoning and ground spices in a food processor or blender and blitz for 30 seconds. Pour the blended mixture over the chicken, cover and refrigerate overnight.

Heat the ghee or butter and oil in a heavy-based shallow pan over a medium heat. Add the whole spices and fry for 30 seconds before adding the onion. Sauté until the onion is soft and translucent.

Add the chicken and the marinade to the pan, combine the ingredients stirring occasionally and fry for 20 minutes. Cover and simmer for 15–20 minutes stirring occasionally. When the mixture has reduced and the oil rises to the surface, stir in the milk.

If necessary, add more milk to keep the chicken moist and well coated with the sauce. Mix the cream and fresh coriander into the sauce and heat through.

Perfect with Sweet and Sour Mango Chutney (page 144) and Favourite Mixed Vegetable Rice (page 125).

The world's favourite, and ours too!

Murgh Tikka
Chicken Tikka

500 g (1 lb) skinless chicken breast fillets, cut into bite-sized pieces

¼ teaspoon salt (or to taste)

Juice of ½ lemon

4 tablespoons roughly chopped fresh coriander

4 garlic cloves, roughly chopped

4 cm (1½ inch) piece of ginger, roughly chopped

2 green chillies, deseeded and roughly chopped

200 ml (7 fl oz) Greek yogurt

½ teaspoon ground nutmeg

1 tablespoon oil

25 g (1 oz) butter or ghee, melted

To finish
Lemon wedges

SERVES 4

FROM YOUR SPICE BOX
GROUND SPICES

½ teaspoon (1 spice spoon) chilli

1 teaspoon (2 spice spoons) coriander

½ teaspoon (1 spice spoon) cumin

½ teaspoon (1 spice spoon) garam masala

½ teaspoon (1 spice spoon) ginger

Rub the chicken with salt and drizzle over the lemon juice. Set aside.

To make the marinade, put the ground spices with the rest of the ingredients except the butter or ghee in a food processor or blender and blitz until smooth.

Pour the marinade mixture over the chicken, cover and leave to marinate in the fridge overnight.

Preheat the oven to 190°C/375°F/Gas mark 5.

Transfer the chicken and the marinade to a roasting tray and cover with foil, sealing the edges firmly. Cook in the preheated oven for 25–30 minutes – don't let it dry out.

Remove the foil and baste the chicken pieces with the butter or ghee. Return to the oven for the chicken to brown for a further 20 minutes.

Serve with lemon wedges, fresh green salad and Chapatis (page 139) or Flatbread Wraps (page 142).

This can also be cooked on the barbecue and served hot, or eaten cold in wraps drizzled with Coriander Chutney (page 145).

Murgh Rogan Josh
Chicken Rogan Josh

3 tablespoons natural yogurt

A pinch of saffron threads

500 g (1 lb) skinless chicken breast fillets, cut into bite-sized pieces

400 g (14 oz) tinned plum tomatoes

4 tablespoons oil

2 garlic cloves, crushed

2.5 cm (1 inch) piece of ginger, grated

2 onions, finely chopped

2 tablespoons tomato purée

200 g (7 oz) fresh tomatoes, skinned and chopped

2 tablespoons finely chopped fresh coriander, plus extra to finish

Salt and freshly ground black pepper

To finish

Fresh coriander leaves

SERVES 4

FROM YOUR SPICE BOX

WHOLE SPICES

2 bay leaves

3 cardamom pods, crushed

2.5 cm (1 inch) cinnamon stick

½ teaspoon (1 spice spoon) cumin seeds

2 cloves, ground

GROUND SPICES

¾ teaspoon (1½ spice spoons) garam masala

½ teaspoon (1 spice spoon) cumin

1 teaspoon (2 spice spoons) ginger

1 teaspoon (2 spice spoons) fennel

1½ teaspoons (3 spice spoons) chilli

½ teaspoon (1 spice spoon) coriander

Mix together the yogurt, saffron, salt and pepper with ¼ teaspoon (½ spice spoon) of the garam masala in a large bowl. Add the chicken to the yogurt marinade. Coat well, cover and leave to marinate for at least 2 hours or more in the fridge.

Separate the tinned plum tomatoes from their juice and blitz to a smooth purée in a food processor or blender. Leave to one side with the juice

Heat the oil in a heavy-based saucepan over a medium heat and add the whole spices. Fry the spices for 30 seconds before adding the garlic, ginger and onions. Fry for a further 5–7 minutes or until the onions are soft and lightly browned.

Add the marinated chicken mixture and stir to combine all the ingredients. Cover and simmer for 8–10 minutes, stirring occasionally. When the mixture has reduced and the oil rises to the surface, uncover and begin to fry the chicken pieces by turning them in the oil until light brown.

Add the rest of the ground spices, except the garam masala. Add the tomato purée, chopped fresh tomatoes and the puréed tomatoes. Mix well for 2–3 minutes and then add the juice from the puréed tomatoes and 250 ml (8 fl oz) water. Stir, cover and cook over a medium–low heat for 15–20 minutes or until the chicken is tender and the sauce is thick.

Stir the remaining garam masala from the ground spices into the sauce before then serving and add fresh coriander leaves.

Serve with Basmati Rice (page 120) and Naan bread (page 138).

Murgh Kali Mirch
Black Pepper Chicken

2 tablespoons lemon juice

3 teaspoons freshly ground black pepper

½ teaspoon salt (or to taste)

500 g (1 lb) skinless chicken breast fillets, cut into bite-sized pieces

4 cm (1½ inch) piece of ginger, roughly chopped

5 garlic cloves, roughly chopped

3 tablespoons oil

2 large onions, finely chopped

2 whole green chillies, pierced

1 tablespoon butter or ghee

6 tablespoons chopped fresh coriander, chopped

SERVES 4

FROM YOUR SPICE BOX

WHOLE SPICES

2 bay leaves

2 cardamom pods, crushed

3 cm (1¼ inches) cinnamon stick

2 cloves

½ teaspoon (1 spice spoon) cumin seeds

GROUND SPICES

½ teaspoon (1 spice spoon) ginger

½ teaspoon (1 spice spoon) turmeric

To finish

Fresh coriander leaves, chopped

Mix together the ground spices, lemon juice, 1 teaspoon of the black pepper and the salt in a small bowl to make a paste.

Put the chicken in a large bowl and rub the paste over the surface of the chicken. Cover and leave to marinate for 2 hours or more in the fridge.

Put the ginger and garlic in a food processor or blender and blitz to a smooth paste (or use a pestle and mortar). Set aside.

Heat the oil in a heavy-based saucepan over a medium heat and add the whole spices and the remaining black pepper. Fry for 30 seconds.

Add the diced onion and ginger–garlic paste and sauté until the onion is soft and translucent.

Stir in the marinated chicken mixture and green chillies. Mix well to combine all the ingredients. Cover and cook for 20 minutes over a low heat, stirring occasionally, until the chicken pieces are tender.

Add the butter or ghee and cook for a further 5 minutes. Pour 100 ml (3½ fl oz) water over the chicken, mix well and bring to the boil before mixing the fresh coriander into the sauce.

Sprinkle with fresh coriander leaves before serving.

Serve with plain Basmati Rice (page 120) and Aubergines in Tomato Sauce (page 96).

Crispy Lemon Chicken

1.5 kg (3 lb) chicken
  drumsticks and thighs
25 g (1 oz) butter
1 large egg, beaten
200–250 g (7–8 oz) dried
  breadcrumbs
Oil, for frying

For the marinade

3 tablespoons lemon juice
3 chicken stock cubes,
  crumbled
6 cm (2½ inch) piece of ginger,
  grated
8 garlic cloves, crushed
2 green chillies, deseeded and
  chopped
A small handful fresh
  coriander, finely chopped
150 ml (¼ pint) Greek yogurt
1 small onion, finely chopped
1 teaspoon freshly ground
  black pepper
2 tablespoons butter

SERVES 6–8

FROM YOUR SPICE BOX

WHOLE SPICES
4 cloves
4 bay leaves
1 stick of cinnamon

GROUND SPICES
1½ teaspoons (3 spice spoons)
  chilli
1½ teaspoons (3 spice spoons)
  coriander
½ teaspoon (1 spice spoon)
  ginger
1 teaspoon (2 spice spoons)
  cumin

Mix all of the marinade ingredients with the whole spices and the ground spices in a large bowl. Make slits in the chicken and add to the marinade – make sure it is well coated. Cover and leave to marinate for 2–4 hours or overnight.

Heat the butter in a heavy-based pan over a medium–low heat and cook the chicken with all the marinade, covered, for 35–40 minutes, or until the liquid has evaporated and the chicken is tender but still intact. Halfway through the cooking take off the lid. Once cooked, leave to cool.

Heat some oil in a wok or deep saucepan over a medium heat. Take one piece of cooked chicken, dip it into the egg and roll in the breadcrumbs before adding to the pan. Fry until golden brown.

Serve hot with Spicy Tomato Dip (page 148) or Cucumber and Tomato Raita (page 151).

Note: for an extra lemon kick, mix half natural dried breadcrumbs with half lemon-flavoured dried breadcrumbs.

Murgh Dhansak

Chicken Dhansak

60 g (2½ oz) yellow split
  chickpeas (channa dal)
250 g (8 oz) butternut squash,
  peeled and roughly chopped
1 large carrot, finely chopped
3 cauliflower florets
3 tablespoons oil
3–4 fresh or dried curry leaves
  (optional)
4 garlic cloves, crushed
4 cm (1½ inch) piece of ginger,
  grated
1 large onion, finely chopped
500 g (1 lb) skinless chicken
  breast fillets, cut into bite-
  sized pieces
1 large tomato, finely chopped
1 tablespoon tomato purée
3 tablespoons finely chopped
  fresh coriander, plus extra
  to finish
2 green chillies, deseeded and
  chopped
Salt

To finish
Fresh coriander leaves,
  chopped

SERVES 4

FROM YOUR SPICE BOX
WHOLE SPICES
¼ teaspoon (½ spice spoon)
  cumin seeds
2 cloves, ground
4 cm (1½ inch) cinnamon stick
2 bay leaves

GROUND SPICES
½ teaspoon (1 spice spoon)
  fennel
¼ teaspoon (½ spice spoon)
  cumin
½ teaspoon (1 spice spoon)
  coriander
½ teaspoon (1 spice spoon)
  ginger
½ teaspoon (1 spice spoon)
  garam masala
½ teaspoon (1 spice spoon)
  chilli
½ teaspoon (1 spice spoon)
  turmeric

Wash the split chickpeas in a sieve and then transfer to a bowl with enough water to fully cover them. Leave to soak overnight.

Place the lentils and the squash, carrot and cauliflower in a large saucepan with 1 litre (1¾ pints) water and bring to the boil. Partially cover and cook over a medium heat until soft. Transfer the lentils and vegetables to a food processor or blender and blitz until smooth. Set aside.

Heat the oil in a heavy-based saucepan over a medium heat and add the whole spices and the curry leaves (if using). Fry for 30 seconds before adding the garlic, ginger and onion. Continue to fry until the onion is light brown in colour.

Add the chicken and fry for 2–3 minutes. Cover and cook for 10 minutes, stirring occasionally, until golden brown.

Temporarily remove from the heat and add the ground spices, salt, tomato and tomato purée and cook for a further 5 minutes. Reduce the heat, pour in the lentil and vegetable purée and 250 ml (8 fl oz) water. Cover and simmer for 20–25 minutes.

Mix in the chopped coriander and green chillies. If the sauce is still quite thick add more water as necessary. Sprinkle with some chopped coriander before serving.

Serve with Roasted New Potatoes with Sesame Seeds (page 94), Mushroom Rice (page 126) and/or Pan-fried Potato Flatbread (page 143). The Walnut and Mint Chutney (page 146) is a refreshing accompaniment.

We regard this as the ultimate wholesome comfort food. This dish can also be made with lamb – just adjust the cooking times as lamb takes longer to cook.

Murgh Aur Aam
Mango Chicken

3 tablespoons oil

4–5 curry leaves

1 large onion, finely chopped

4 garlic cloves, crushed

2 cm (³/₄ inch) piece of ginger, grated

1 whole green chilli, pierced

500 g (1 lb) skinless chicken breast fillets, cut into bite-sized pieces

1 mango (not too ripe), peeled and roughly chopped

200 ml (7 fl oz) coconut milk

Salt and freshly ground black pepper

To finish

Fresh coriander leaves

SERVES 4

FROM YOUR SPICE BOX

WHOLE SPICES

3 cardamom pods, crushed

2 bay leaves

¹/₂ teaspoon (1 spice spoon) cumin seeds

4cm (1¹/₂ inch) cinnamon stick

GROUND SPICES

1 teaspoon (2 spice spoons) coriander

¹/₂ teaspoon (1 spice spoon) turmeric

¹/₂ teaspoon (1 spice spoon) chilli

¹/₂ teaspoon (1 spice spoon) cumin

Heat a heavy-based saucepan over a medium heat, add the oil, the whole spices and the curry leaves and fry for 30 seconds.

Add the onion, garlic, ginger and fresh green chilli and fry until lightly browned.

Add the ground spices and seasoning and cook for a few minutes more.

Add the chicken and fry for 10 minutes or until the chicken is well coated with the spices.

Set aside 1–2 tablespoons of the mango to use as a garnish. Put the remaining mango in a food processor or blender and blitz until smooth. Strain and discard any fibres (optional).

Put the puréed mango in a bowl and add the coconut milk. Mix until you have a uniform colour.

Add the mango and coconut purée to the chicken. Cook, covered over a low heat for 15 minutes or until the chicken is tender. Sprinkle with fresh coriander before serving.

Serve with Favourite Mixed Vegetable Rice (page 125), Saffron Rice (page 122), Naan bread (page 138) and Cucumber and Tomato Raita (page 151).

Murgh Jalfrezi
Chicken Jalfrezi

3 tablespoons butter

2 tablespoons oil

2 garlic cloves, crushed

2 cm (¾ inch) piece of ginger, grated

2 onions, finely chopped, plus 1 small onion, thinly sliced

2 shallots, finely chopped

3 tomatoes, finely chopped

1½ teaspoons freshly ground black pepper

500 g (1 lb) skinless chicken breast fillets, cut into bite-sized pieces

200 g (7 oz) mixed peppers

Salt

¼ teaspoon ground cinnamon

SERVES 4

FROM YOUR SPICE BOX

WHOLE SPICES

2 bay leaves

½ teaspoon (1 spice spoon) cumin seeds

GROUND SPICES

½ teaspoon (1 spice spoon) chilli

½ teaspoon (1 spice spoon) fennel

½ teaspoon (1 spice spoon) coriander

½ teaspoon (1 spice spoon) ginger

½ teaspoon (1 spice spoon) cumin

¾ teaspoon (1½ spice spoons) garam masala

Heat 2 tablespoons of the butter with the oil in a heavy-based saucepan over a medium heat and add the bay leaves and cumin seeds from the whole spices. Fry for 30 seconds.

Add the garlic, ginger, chopped onions, shallots and 2 of the finely chopped tomatoes then stir for 1 minute.

Add all of the ground spices (leaving ¼ teaspoon or ½ spice spoon of garam masala and the ground cinnamon for later), 1 teaspoon black pepper and some salt. Cover and cook for about 7–8 minutes or until the tomatoes are soft.

Add the chicken to the pan and mix well. Cover and leave to cook for 20 minutes.

Heat the remaining 1 tablespoon butter in another saucepan and add the sliced onion, peppers and remaining tomato, a pinch of salt, the remaining garam masala, the ground cinnamon and the remaining black pepper. Fry for 5–7 minutes.

Add this mixture to the pan with the chicken and cook for 2–3 minutes. Finish with chopped spring onion and fresh coriander before serving.

Serve with Potatoes with Peas (page 98) and Basmati Rice (page 120) and/or Deep-fried Bread (page 140).

Murgh Korma
Chicken Korma

6 tablespoons oil

500 g (1 lb) skinless chicken breast fillets, cut into bite-sized pieces

2 cm (³/₄ inch) piece of ginger, roughly chopped

2 garlic cloves, roughly chopped

1 onion, roughly chopped

2 green chillies, deseeded and chopped

¹/₂ teaspoon salt (or to taste)

300 ml (¹/₂ pint) natural yogurt

20 g (³/₄ oz) ground almonds

25 g (1 oz) unsalted cashews, ground

3 tablespoons thick single cream

2 tablespoons fresh coriander leaves

To finish

Fresh coriander leaves, finely chopped

¹/₂ teaspoon saffron threads, soaked in 1 tablespoon warm milk (optional)

SERVES 4

FROM YOUR SPICE BOX

WHOLE SPICES

1 bay leaf

3 cm (1¹/₂ inch) cinnamon stick

1 clove

2 cardamom pods, crushed

GROUND SPICES

¹/₂ teaspoon (1 spice spoon) chilli

1 teaspoon (2 spice spoons) coriander

¹/₂ teaspoon (1 spice spoon) cumin

¹/₂ teaspoon (1 spice spoon) ginger

1 teaspoon (2 spice spoons) garam masala

Heat half the quantity of oil in a heavy-based saucepan over a medium heat. Add the chicken and fry for 3 minutes stirring occasionally. Remove the chicken with a slotted spoon and set aside.

Put the ginger, garlic, onion, fresh green chilli and salt in a food processor or blender and blitz for 30 seconds to a coarse paste. Set aside.

Whisk together the yogurt, almonds, cashews, cream and 100 ml (3¹/₂ fl oz) water. Set aside.

Pour the remaining oil into the saucepan and fry the whole spices for 30 seconds. Add the blended paste to the pan and fry for 3 minutes. Add the chicken and all of the ground spices except the garam masala. Fry for a further 2–3 minutes.

Reduce the heat and fold in the whisked yogurt mixture. Cover and simmer for 25 minutes with occasional stirring. Mix in the fresh coriander leaves and garam masala and heat through for a further 1–2 minutes.

On serving, if the sauce requires thinning, add 100 ml (3¹/₂ fl oz) water and bring to the boil. Drizzle the saffron milk (if using) over the chicken and sprinkle with finely chopped coriander leaves before serving.

Serve with Basmati Rice (page 120) or Naan bread (page 138).

Zafrani Murgh

Chicken in a Saffron and Yogurt Sauce

2 tablespoons oil
500–600 g (1–1¼ lb) skinless chicken breast fillets, cut into bite-sized pieces
125 ml (4 fl oz) natural yogurt
125 ml (4 fl oz) milk
5–7 saffron threads
1 whole green chilli, pierced
2 tablespoons single cream
Salt and freshly ground black pepper

SERVES 4

FROM YOUR SPICE BOX
WHOLE SPICES
2 bay leaves
½ teaspoon (1 spice spoon) cumin seeds
3 cardamom pods, crushed
4cm (1½ inch) cinnamon stick
1 clove, ground

GROUND SPICES
¾ teaspoon (1½ spice spoons) ginger
1 teaspoon (2 spice spoons) turmeric
½ teaspoon (1 spice spoon) coriander
¼ teaspoon (½ spice spoon) cumin
1 teaspoon (2 spice spoons) fennel
¼ teaspoon (½ spice spoon) garam masala

Heat the oil in a heavy-based saucepan over a medium heat and add the whole spices. Fry for 30 seconds then add the chicken and 150 ml (¼ pint) water.

Cover and cook for 8–10 minutes or until all the water has evaporated. Fry until the chicken is light brown.

Remove from the heat momentarily and add the ground spices, except for the garam masala, followed by the salt and pepper.

Whisk the yogurt, milk and saffron threads together in a small bowl.

Return the saucepan to the heat and add the yogurt mixture and the whole chilli, stirring continuously to stop it from curdling.

Stir in 350 ml (12 fl oz) water. Cook and cover for 5 minutes, or until the chicken is tender. Mix in the garam masala and swirl in the single cream.

Serve with Broccoli with Cumin and Ginger (page 92), Basmati Rice (page 120) and/or Chapatis (page 139). The Spicy Tomato Dip (page 148) is the perfect chutney to accompany.

This mild chicken dish has a lovely sweetness that comes from the yogurt. It's a great one for introducing children to Indian food or for adults who don't want anything too spicy.

Gosht

Lamb

Tabakh-Maaz

Lamb Chops Braised in Saffron Milk

2 tablespoons oil, plus extra for shallow frying

A large pinch of asafoetida

1 star anise

8 lamb loin chops, weighing about 850 g (1¾ lb) in total

¼ teaspoon nutmeg

1–1.5 litres (1¾–2½ pints) whole milk

5–6 saffron threads

1 tablespoon ground almonds

Salt and freshly ground black pepper

To finish

Flaked almonds

Edible silver leaf (optional)

SERVES 4

FROM YOUR SPICE BOX

WHOLE SPICES

½ teaspoon (1 spice spoon) cumin seeds

2 bay leaves

4 cm (1½ inch) cinnamon stick

3 cardamom pods, crushed

2 cloves, ground

GROUND SPICES

¾ teaspoon (1½ spice spoons) ginger

¼ teaspoon (½ spice spoon) cumin

1 teaspoon (2 spice spoons) fennel

Heat the oil in a large heavy-based saucepan over a medium heat and add the whole spices from your spice box plus the asafoetida and the star anise. Fry for 30 seconds.

Curl each lamb chop into a neat shape and secure with cocktail sticks. Add the lamb chops and a pinch of salt to the saucepan and lightly brown the meat.

Mix in the ground spices from your spice box, plus the nutmeg then add the milk, saffron threads and ground almonds. Bring to the boil, stirring constantly. As the sauce thickens, it may appear to curdle – don't be alarmed, this is normal.

Reduce the heat, partially cover and cook for 1–1½ hours, stirring occasionally, or until the meat is tender and almost no liquid remains. Leave to cool, uncovered.

When ready to eat, take out each chop and shallow fry in batches until golden. Strain the sauce to remove any whole spices (you can use them to decoratet the finished dish) and add a little milk or water to make it a pouring consistency – heat and serve separately in a small bowl.

Remove the cocktail sticks from the meat before serving. Decorate with flaked almonds and edible silver leaf (if using).

Serve hot with the sauce, Lemon Rice (page 121) and Mint and Yogurt Chutney (page 152).

This dish reminds us all of the first wedding we went to as children in Kashmir. It was served in ceremonial style on large silver platters.

Gosht ka Kalia

Yogurt-marinated Lamb

200 ml (7 fl oz) Greek yogurt

500 g (1 lb) boneless leg of lamb, cut into bite-sized pieces

3 tablespoons oil

1 tablespoon butter

Salt and freshly ground black pepper

SERVES 4

FROM YOUR SPICE BOX

WHOLE SPICES

2 bay leaves

3 cardamom pods, crushed

2 cloves

½ teaspoon (1 spice spoon) cumin seeds

2 cm (¾ inch) cinnamon stick

GROUND SPICES

½ teaspoon (1 spice spoon) cumin

1½ teaspoons (3 spice spoons) fennel

1 teaspoon (2 spice spoons) ginger

1 teaspoon (2 spice spoons) turmeric

½ teaspoon (1 spice spoon) garam masala

Marinate half the quantity of yogurt with a pinch of salt and all of the ground spices, except the garam masala, in a large bowl. Add the lamb and mix thoroughly so that the meat is well coated. Cover and refrigerate for 2 hours or more.

Heat the oil in a heavy-based saucepan over a medium heat and add the whole spices. Fry for 30–40 seconds before adding the marinated lamb mixture.

Partially cover and simmer, stirring occasionally, for 20–25 minutes or until the oil separates from the meat. Add the butter.

Whisk the remaining yogurt with 450 ml (¾ pint) water in a bowl to a smooth consistency and then add it to the meat.

Gently bring to the boil stirring continuously. Cover and simmer for 25–30 minutes stirring occasionally so that the lamb does not stick to the bottom of the saucepan.

If the meat requires more time to soften, add another 150 ml (¼ pint) water and simmer for a further 10 minutes.

Add a twist of black pepper and the garam masala and mix well into the sauce.

Perfect for lunch or supper with Tomato Salad (page 37), Green Beans (page 105) and Basmati Rice (page 120).

Gosht Rogan Josh
Lamb Rogan Josh

4 tablespoons natural yogurt

500 g (1 lb) boneless leg of lamb, cut into bite-sized pieces

4 tablespoons oil

2 garlic cloves, crushed

½ teaspoon sugar

2 tablespoons tomato purée

200 g (7 oz) tinned plum tomatoes, chopped

Salt and freshly ground black pepper

To finish

Fresh coriander leaves, finely chopped

SERVES 4

FROM YOUR SPICE BOX

WHOLE SPICES

2 bay leaves

3 cardamom pods, crushed

4 cm (1½ inch) cinnamon stick

2 cloves

½ teaspoon (1 spice spoon) cumin seeds

GROUND SPICES

1 teaspoon (2 spice spoons) garam masala

1½ teaspoons (3 spice spoons) chilli

1 teaspoon (2 spice spoons) coriander

1½ teaspoons (3 spice spoons) fennel

1 teaspoon (2 spice spoons) ginger

½ teaspoon (1 spice spoon) cumin

Make a marinade using the yogurt, half of the garam masala from the ground spices and some seasoning in a large bowl. Add the lamb to the marinade and mix thoroughly so that the meat is well coated. Cover and refrigerate for 2 hours or more.

Heat the oil in a large heavy-based saucepan over a medium heat. Add the whole spices and fry for 30 seconds. Add the garlic and fry for 30 seconds before stirring in the marinated meat pieces.

Cover and cook for 20–25 minutes, or until the oil begins to separate from the meat. Brown the meat pieces evenly in the oil by turning them frequently for 5 minutes. Do not worry if at this stage some of the mixture sticks to the bottom of the saucepan.

Hold the saucepan handle upwards at an angle so that the oil collects to one side and add the sugar. Caramelize to a deep brown colour. Lower the saucepan down to its original position, gently swirling it to spread the oil.

Add the rest of the ground spices, except the remaining garam masala and add 4 tablespoons water. Turn the meat in the spices for a few minutes before adding the tomato purée, tomatoes and 450 ml (¾ pint) water.

Cover and simmer for 25–30 minutes, stirring frequently to prevent sticking, while reducing to a thick sauce. Mix the garam masala into the sauce. Finish with fresh coriander leaves and serve with Potatoes with Okra (page 109) and Basmati Rice (page 120).

This is the king of all lamb dishes and Sereena's favourite, especially when Alexa or our Mum makes it for her!

Aloo Gosht

Lamb with Spiced Potatoes

4 tablespoons oil

300 g (10 oz) small new
  potatoes, scrubbed and
  halved

A pinch of asafoetida

3 garlic cloves, crushed

2 cm (³/₄ inch) piece of ginger,
  grated

2 onions, finely chopped

2 shallots, finely chopped

500 g (1 lb) lean boneless leg
  of lamb, cut into bite-sized
  pieces

2 tomatoes, finely chopped

Salt and freshly ground black
  pepper

To finish

Fresh coriander, finely chopped

Spring onions, chopped

SERVES 4

FROM YOUR SPICE BOX

WHOLE SPICES

1 bay leaf

½ teaspoon (1 spice spoon)
  cumin seeds

4 cm (1½ inch) cinnamon stick

GROUND SPICES

½ teaspoon (1 spice spoon)
  turmeric

1 teaspoon (2 spice spoons)
  ginger

1¼ teaspoons (2½ spice
  spoons) fennel

¼ teaspoon (½ spice spoon)
  cumin

1 teaspoon (2 spice spoons)
  chilli

½ teaspoon (1 spice spoon)
  garam masala

Heat the oil in a heavy-based saucepan over a medium heat and fry the potatoes until golden brown on all sides. Remove with a slotted spoon and leave to one side.

Using the same saucepan add the whole spices, asafoetida, garlic, ginger, onions and shallots. Fry until the onion mixture is lightly browned. Add the lamb and a pinch of salt and fry for a further 5–6 minutes or until browned. Add 400 ml (14 fl oz) water and cover and cook until the lamb is tender and all the liquid has evaporated. Fry the lamb for a further 1–2 minutes.

Add the ground spices, except for the garam masala, and the tomatoes. Mix well, cover and cook for 5–7 minutes or until the lamb is well coated with the spices.

Add 600 ml (1 pint) water and bring to the boil. Cover and simmer for 7–8 minutes or until half the sauce remains.

Return the potatoes to the pan, cover and cook until the potatoes are just soft. There should be enough sauce to cover the lamb and the potatoes – add a little more water if needed.

Mix in the garam masala and garnish with finely chopped fresh coriander and spring onions.

Serve with Saffron Rice (page 122) and Naan bread (page 138) and accompany with Butternut Squash with Cumin and Mint (page 99).

Our first memory of this dish was eating it on our Uncle's houseboat on Dal Lake, Srinagar.

Kashmiri Matz

Kashmiri Lamb in a Chilli Sauce

For the matz (lamb mince)

2 cm (³/₄ inch) piece of ginger,
  roughly chopped
4 garlic cloves, roughly chopped
500 g (1 lb) lamb mince
1 tablespoon finely chopped
  fresh coriander
2 tablespoons natural yogurt
¼ teaspoon salt (or to taste)
1 egg yolk
½ small onion, finely chopped
1 tablespoon oil, plus extra
  for oiling

SERVES 4

FROM YOUR SPICE BOX

WHOLE SPICES

3 cardamom pods, crushed

GROUND SPICES

1 teaspoon (2 spice spoons) chilli
1 teaspoon (2 spice spoons)
  coriander
³/₄ teaspoon (1½ spice spoons)
  cumin
1 teaspoon (2 spice spoons)
  fennel
1 teaspoon (2 spice spoons)
  garam masala
1 teaspoon (2 spice spoons)
  ginger

For the matz

Put the ginger and garlic in a food processor or blender and blitz to a smooth paste (or use a pestle and mortar).

Lightly oil a bowl and place the mince in the centre. Add half the ginger–garlic paste (set aside the other half for the sauce), all of the rest of the ingredients for the matz and the whole and ground spices.

With wet hands, divide the mince mixture into 16 equal balls. On a lightly oiled surface, roll each mince ball into a sausage-oval shape of 6 cm (2¼ inches) length. Pinch the ends to seal the matz. Set aside while preparing the sauce.

For the sauce

Heat the oil in a shallow pan over a medium heat and add the whole spices and the reserved ginger–garlic paste from the matz steps. Fry for 30 seconds before adding 250 ml (8 fl oz) water and bring to the boil. Gently place the prepared matz, one by one, into the boiling water.

Cover and simmer for 25–30 minutes or until the water reduces and only the oil remains. Hold the saucepan handle upwards slightly at an angle so that all the oil collects to one side and add the sugar. Caramelize to a deep brown colour and then lower the saucepan down to its original position, gently swirling it to spread the oil.

Add the tomato purée, chopped tomatoes, salt and ground spices except the garam masala. Cover and cook for 5–7 minutes stirring gently at regular intervals and taking care not to fragment the matz pieces.

Pour in 750 ml (1¼ pints) water and cook for a further 20 minutes, reducing it to a runny sauce. Mix in the garam masala.

Finish with fresh coriander and finely chopped onion.

Serve with Lemon Rice (page 121) and Potatoes with Okra (page 109).

Everyone's favourite – we can't get enough of these! As kids we always pushed the limit and asked for 'just one more please, Mum!'

FROM YOUR SPICE BOX

WHOLE SPICES

1 bay leaf

2 cardamom pods, crushed

¼ teaspoon (½ spice spoon) cumin seeds

GROUND SPICES

1 teaspoon (2 spice spoons) chilli

1 teaspoon (2 spice spoons) coriander

¼ teaspoon (½ spice spoon) cumin

1 teaspoon (2 spice spoons) fennel

1 teaspoon (2 spice spoons) ginger

½ teaspoon (1 spice spoon) turmeric

¼ teaspoon (½ spice spoon) garam masala

For the chilli sauce

2 tablespoons oil

1 litre (1¾ pints) water

½ teaspoon sugar

3 tablespoons tomato purée

4 tablespoons chopped tomatoes

¼ teaspoon salt (or to taste)

To finish

Fresh coriander, finely chopped

½ small onion, finely chopped

Sukhe Tamatar Walla Ka Gosht

Lamb with Sun-dried Tomatoes

3 tablespoons oil

3 garlic cloves, crushed

2 cm (³/₄ inch) piece of ginger, grated

500 g (1 lb) boneless leg of lamb, cut into bite-sized pieces

300 g (10 oz) sun-dried tomatoes in oil, drained

1 tablespoon butter

3 tablespoons finely chopped fresh coriander

1 whole green chilli, pierced

Salt

SERVES 4

FROM YOUR SPICE BOX

WHOLE SPICES

¹/₂ teaspoon (1 spice spoon) cumin seeds

2 bay leaves

1 clove, ground

3–4 cm (1¹/₄–1¹/₂ inch) cinnamon stick

GROUND SPICES

1 teaspoon (2 spice spoons) chilli

³/₄ teaspoon (1¹/₂ spice spoons) fennel

¹/₂ teaspoon (1 spice spoon) ginger

¹/₂ teaspoon (1 spice spoon) turmeric

¹/₄ teaspoon (¹/₂ spice spoon) cumin

¹/₂ teaspoon (1 spice spoon) garam masala

Heat the oil in a heavy-based saucepan over a medium heat and add the whole spices. Fry for 30 seconds then add the garlic, ginger and lamb and a pinch of salt. Cover and cook for 10 minutes, or until the oil separates from the lamb.

Fry the meat for a few minutes until lightly browned then add 750 ml (1¹/₄ pints) water.

Cover and cook for 25 minutes. Stir and continue cooking until the water has evaporated and the lamb is soft, stirring occasionally.

Add the tomatoes and ground spices and stir well. Add 100 ml (3¹/₂ fl oz) water and the whole green chilli and cook for a further minute.

Stir in the butter and fresh coriander and mix well.

Accompany with Green Beans (page 105), Favourite Mixed Vegetable Rice (page 125), Chapatis (page 139) and Walnut and Mint Chutney (page 146).

During the summer months in Kashmir we would pick the ripe tomatoes and dry them to preserve for the winter ahead. The sun-dried tomatoes add a wonderful richness and flavour to the lamb – Alexa's favourite.

Kheema Matar

Minced Lamb with Tomatoes and Peas

150 g (5 oz) frozen peas

3 tablespoons oil

4 garlic cloves, crushed

3 cm (1¼ inch) piece of ginger, grated

2 large onions, finely chopped

500 g (1 lb) lamb mince

2 tablespoons tomato purée

¼ teaspoon salt (or to taste)

200 g (7 oz) tinned chopped tomatoes

200 ml (7 fl oz) sieved tomatoes (passata)

1 teaspoon dried mint leaves or 1 tablespoon chopped fresh mint leaves

4 tablespoons finely chopped fresh coriander, plus extra to finish

SERVES 4

FROM YOUR SPICE BOX

WHOLE SPICES

2 bay leaves

½ teaspoon (1 spice spoon) cumin seeds

GROUND SPICES

1 teaspoon (2 spice spoons) chilli

2 teaspoons (4 spice spoons) coriander

½ teaspoon (1 spice spoon) cumin

1½ teaspoons (3 spice spoons) ginger

1 teaspoon (2 spice spoons) turmeric

½ teaspoon (1 spice spoon) garam masala

Boil the peas in water for 5 minutes, drain and refresh in cold water. Set aside.

Heat the oil in a large heavy-based saucepan over a medium heat and add the whole spices. When the seeds begin to sizzle, stir in the garlic and ginger and fry for 30 seconds.

Set aside 1 tablespoon of the chopped onions for a garnish. Add the rest of the onions to the pan and sauté for 3–4 minutes before adding the lamb. Stir frequently for 10 minutes or until the mince is light brown and crumbly.

Remove momentarily from the heat and mix in the ground spices, except the garam masala, followed by the tomato purée and salt.

Cook for 5 minutes, stirring occasionally, before adding the chopped tomatoes and passata. Cook for a further 7 minutes, stirring in a couple of tablespoons of water from time to time to prevent the meat from sticking to the bottom of the saucepan.

Add 250 ml (8 fl oz) water, cover and simmer for 20–25 minutes or until reduced to a fairly thick sauce.

Before serving, add the peas, mint leaves, fresh coriander and garam masala and bring back to the boil. Remove from the heat.

Finish with the reserved chopped onion and fresh coriander leaves.

Serve with Basmati Rice (page 120) or Naan bread (page 138).

Our Dad made this once when Mum was in hospital. We watched him like a hawk in case he tripped up, but luckily for him this is an easy dish to make.

Bhuna Masala Gosht

Pan-fried Garlic and Chilli Lamb

2 tablespoons oil

1 tablespoon butter

2 garlic cloves, crushed

600 g (1¼ lb) lean boneless leg of lamb, cut into bite-sized pieces

Salt

2 little gem lettuces, finely shredded, to serve

To finish

Fresh coriander, chopped

Green and red chillies, finely sliced

SERVES 4

FROM YOUR SPICE BOX

WHOLE SPICES

½ teaspoon (1 spice spoon) cumin seeds

2–3 cardamom pods, crushed

2 bay leaves

2 cloves, finely ground

GROUND SPICES

½ teaspoon (1 spice spoon) ginger

½ teaspoon (1 spice spoon) chilli

½ teaspoon (1 spice spoon) garam masala

Heat the oil and butter in a heavy-based shallow frying pan over a medium heat and add the whole spices and garlic.

Fry for 30 seconds, then add the lamb and a pinch of salt. Seal the lamb for a few minutes, then add 900 ml (1½ pints) water and stir.

Cover and cook, stirring occasionally, for 35–40 minutes, or until the lamb is tender and the water has evaporated. Cook a little longer if the lamb is still not tender and add more water as necessary.

Remove from the heat, mix in the ground spices and 1 tablespoon water then stir for 20–30 seconds. Serve on a bed of shredded lettuce.

Serve hot with Naan bread (page 138) and accompany with Pan-fried Fruity Aubergine (page 103) and Saffron Rice (page 122).

Note: keep the lamb moist by adding a little water towards the end of the cooking time.

Priya serves this as a starter with a fresh tomato salad.

Macchli Aur Jhinga

Fish and Prawns

Annanasi Jhinga
Tandoori Prawns with Pineapple

500 g (1 lb) raw king prawns,
  tails left on

1½ teaspoons lemon juice

2 cm (¾ inch) piece of ginger,
  grated

3 garlic cloves, crushed

2 teaspoons oil, plus extra for
  the skewers

1 tablespoon Greek yogurt

A good pinch of nutmeg

½ teaspoon freshly ground
  black pepper

300 g (10 oz) pineapple, cubed

2 tablespoons butter, melted

Salt

Lemon or lime wedges,
  to finish

12 metal skewers or wooden
  bamboo sticks soaked in cold
  water for 30 minutes

SERVES 6–8

FROM YOUR SPICE BOX
GROUND SPICES

½ teaspoon (1 spice spoon)
  turmeric

¼ teaspoon (½ spice spoon)
  chilli

½ teaspoon (1 spice spoon)
  ginger

¼ teaspoon (½ spice spoon)
  cumin

½ teaspoon (1 spice spoon)
  garam masala

Put the prawns in a sieve and sprinkle over a little salt, the turmeric from the ground spices and a squeeze of lemon juice.

Leave to one side for 15 minutes and then wash the prawns under a gentle stream of water and dry between sheets of kitchen paper.

Put the ginger, garlic, oil, yogurt, nutmeg, salt and pepper and the remaining ground spices in a food processor or blender and blitz to a smooth paste. Add this to the prawns and mix to ensure they are evenly coated. Leave to marinate in the fridge for 30 minutes until you are ready to serve.

Heat the grill on a medium–high setting.

Rub the skewers with a little oil and alternately thread the prawns and pineapple chunks on each one – dividing the ingredients equally between the skewers.

Cook under the hot grill for around 4–6 minutes, turning once, until the prawns are cooked and browned. Baste with a little melted butter half way through cooking.

Serve hot with lemon or lime wedges as a starter or snack, or as a main dish with Spicy Okra (page 117) and Basmati Rice (page 120).

Anything tandoori is healthy, especially with fruit mixed in. We find these are also really tasty cooked on a barbecue.

Masala Jhinga
Chilli Prawns

3 cm (1¼ inch) piece of root
   ginger, roughly chopped
4 garlic cloves, roughly chopped
4 tablespoons roughly chopped
   fresh coriander
1 onion, roughly chopped
1 whole green chilli
3 tablespoons unsalted butter
500 g (1 lb) raw tiger or king
   prawns, peeled and de-veined
2 tablespoons lemon juice
Salt and freshly ground black
   pepper

SERVES 4

FROM YOUR SPICE BOX
WHOLE SPICES
½ teaspoon (1 spice spoon)
   cumin seeds

GROUND SPICES
1 teaspoon (2 spice spoons)
   chilli
1 teaspoon (2 spice spoons)
   ginger

Put the ginger, garlic, fresh coriander, onion, green chilli and seasoning in a food processor or blender and blitz to a smooth paste. Set aside.

Heat the butter in a heavy-based shallow pan over a medium heat and add the whole spice. When the seeds begin to sizzle add the ginger–garlic paste and the prawns.

Fry for 5 minutes before pouring in 125 ml (4 fl oz) water. Stir frequently for 1 minute or until the mixture is fairly dry.

Add the ground spices and lemon juice. Mix well to combine all the ingredients for 30 seconds.

Serve with Favourite Mixed Vegetable Rice (page 125) or in a Flatbread Wrap (page 142) with Sweet and Sour Mango Chutney (page 144).

Adraki Jhinga
Ginger Prawns

5 cm (2 inch) piece of ginger, roughly chopped

2 green chillies, deseeded and chopped

1 tablespoon lemon juice

500 g (1 lb) raw king prawns, peeled and de-veined

3 tablespoons oil

Salt

4 lemon wedges, to serve

SERVES 4

FROM YOUR SPICE BOX
GROUND SPICES

1 teaspoon (2 spice spoons) chilli

1 teaspoon (2 spice spoons) ginger

Put the ginger, green chillies, lemon juice, a pinch of salt and ground spices in a food processor or blender and blitz to a fine paste. Set aside.

Blot the prawns dry with sheets of kitchen paper to absorb any moisture and transfer to a large bowl. Coat them with the ginger paste and set aside for 15 minutes.

Heat the oil in a heavy-based shallow pan over a medium–high heat and fry the marinated prawns for 2 minutes on both sides. Take care not to overcook the prawns as they will become rubbery.

Serve with wedges of lemon and Spicy Tomato Dip (page 148) as a starter.

Malai Jhinga
Creamy Prawns

600 g (1¼ lb) large raw
  prawns, peeled and de-veined
2.5 cm (1 inch) piece of ginger
3 garlic cloves
1 large onion, roughly chopped
3 tablespoons oil
1 whole green chilli
200 ml (7 fl oz) coconut milk
Salt and freshly ground black
  pepper

SERVES 4

FROM YOUR SPICE BOX
WHOLE SPICES

1 bay leaf
5 cm (2 inch) cinnamon stick

GROUND SPICES

1 teaspoon (2 spice spoons)
  turmeric
1 teaspoon (2 spice spoons)
  chilli
½ teaspoon (1 spice spoon)
  garam masala
½ teaspoon (1 spice spoon)
  ginger

Place the prawns in a large bowl and sprinkle with half of the turmeric from the ground spices and a pinch of salt. Set aside for 10–15 minutes before rinsing under a stream of cold water. Dry between sheets of kitchen paper.

Put the ginger, garlic and onion in a food processor or blender and blitz to a coarse paste. Set aside.

Heat the oil in a heavy-based shallow pan over a medium heat and fry the whole spices for 20–30 seconds. Tip in the prawns and fry for 2 minutes. Remove with a slotted spoon and set aside.

Add the onion paste to the pan and sauté for 6–8 minutes stirring occasionally. Remove from the heat momentarily and mix in the ground spices, a pinch of salt and the prawns.

Return to the heat and add 150 ml (¼ pint) water, the green chilli and the coconut milk. Allow to cook for 1 minute without boiling. Season with black pepper.

Serve with Green Beans (page 105), Potatoes and Cauliflower (page 100) and Basmati Rice (page 120).

Sukhi Macchli

Dry Spiced Fish

600 g (1¼ lb) haddock or salmon fillets, skinned and cut into 6 cm (2¼ inch) pieces
1 tablespoon lemon juice
2 cm (¾ inch) piece of ginger, grated
2 garlic cloves, crushed
2 tablespoons oil
1 tablespoon finely chopped fresh coriander
Salt and freshly ground black pepper
Flour, for dusting
Oil, for shallow frying

SERVES 4

FROM YOUR SPICE BOX
GROUND SPICES
1 teaspoon (2 spice spoons) chilli
1 teaspoon (2 spice spoons) coriander
½ teaspoon (1 spice spoon) cumin
½ teaspoon (1 spice spoon) fennel
1 teaspoon (2 spice spoons) turmeric

Drizzle the haddock or salmon with the lemon juice and set aside.

In a large bowl, mix together the ground spices and all the rest of the ingredients.

Add the fish with the lemon juice to the bowl and coat well with the marinade. Cover and leave to marinate for at least 1 hour in the fridge.

Dust each piece of fish with flour and shake off any excess. Shallow fry for 3–4 minutes on each side until the fish is cooked through.

Serve with lemon wedges, Tomato Salad (page 37) and Cumin Potatoes (page 104).

A great alternative to fish and chips.

Nimbu Adraki Macchli

Citrus Fish with Ginger

600 g (1¼ lb) tilapia fish
    fillets, or any firm white fish
Juice of 1 lime
Salt
Oil, for shallow frying

SERVES 6

FROM YOUR SPICE BOX
GROUND SPICES
½ teaspoon (1 spice spoon)
    turmeric
½ teaspoon (1 spice spoon)
    ginger
½ teaspoon (1 spice spoon)
    chilli

Cut each fish fillet into four pieces. Put them in a colander, sprinkle lightly with salt and drizzle over half of the lime juice. Rub in the turmeric from the ground spices and leave the fish to one side for 15 minutes.

Mix together the ground spices with some salt and leave to one side.

Wash the fish under a gentle stream of running water and dry between sheets of kitchen paper.

Heat the oil in a shallow frying pan over a medium heat, and fry the fish fillets until golden.

Remove with a slotted spoon and sprinkle over the remaining ground spices and squeeze over some more lime juice.

Serve hot with Tomato Rice (page 124) and accompany with Pan-fried Fruity Aubergine (page 103).

We all love this – it makes a great midweek supper served with a fresh green salad.

Goan Tuna Macchli

Goan Tuna Steaks

4 tuna steaks, each weighing
about 150 g (5 oz)

2 lemons, grated rind of 1 and
juice of both

2 red chillies, deseeded and
finely chopped

4 tablespoons chopped fresh
coriander

300 ml (½ pint) sieved tomatoes
(passata)

2 cm (¾ inch) piece of ginger,
finely chopped

400 ml (14 fl oz) full fat
coconut milk

2 tablespoons oil

Salt and freshly ground
black pepper

SERVES 4

FROM YOUR SPICE BOX

WHOLE SPICES

1 teaspoon (2 spice spoons)
black mustard seeds

½ teaspoon (1 spice spoon)
cumin seeds

GROUND SPICES

½ teaspoon (1 spice spoon)
chilli

½ teaspoon (1 spice spoon)
cumin

½ teaspoon (1 spice spoon)
coriander

Rinse the tuna steaks under cold water. Drain well and rub with the juice of 1 lemon to remove the fish odour. Rinse again and pat dry with sheets of kitchen paper.

Mix the mustard seeds, cumin seeds, lemon rind, chopped chillies and coriander in a shallow dish, add the tuna and coat well. Cover with cling film and leave to marinate in the fridge for 30 minutes or longer.

For the sauce, put the passata in a saucepan with the ground spices and chopped ginger. Simmer for 3–4 minutes until thick, stirring occasionally. Stir in the coconut milk and cook for 2–3 minutes more. Add the lemon juice and add salt and pepper to taste.

Heat the oil in a large frying pan, add the tuna and cook for 2 minutes until lightly browned on one side, turn over and cook for 1–3 minutes, depending on the thickness and how rare you like your tuna.

Serve with plain Basmati Rice (page 120) and a little sauce drizzled around the tuna. Serve the remaining sauce in a bowl.

This dish evokes memories for Alexa of her first trip to Goa – sitting on the beach eating the freshest tuna drizzled with the delicately flavoured coconut and tomato sauce.

Naryal Dood ki Macchi
Monkfish in Coconut Milk

600 g (1¼ lb) monkfish fillet,
  cut into 6 cm (2¼ inch) pieces
2 tablespoons lemon juice
5 cm (2 inch) piece of ginger,
  roughly chopped
3 garlic cloves
1 onion, roughly chopped
2 green chillies, 1 deseeded and
  1 left whole
2½ tablespoons oil
4 curry leaves (optional)
350 ml (12 fl oz) coconut milk
2 tomatoes, peeled and chopped
2 tablespoons finely chopped
  fresh coriander
Salt and freshly ground black
  pepper

SERVES 4

FROM YOUR SPICE BOX
WHOLE SPICES
2 bay leaves
3 cardamom pods, crushed
2 cloves
5 cm (2 inch) cinnamon stick
½ teaspoon (1 spice spoon)
  mustard seeds

GROUND SPICES
½ teaspoon (1 spice spoon)
  coriander
½ teaspoon (1 spice spoon)
  cumin
¼ teaspoon (½ spice spoon)
  each fennel, garam masala
  and ginger

Place the monkfish on a plate and sprinkle with salt. Drizzle with 1 tablespoon of the lemon juice and set aside for 15–20 minutes.

Gently rinse the fish under cold water and pat dry between sheets of kitchen paper. Set aside.

Put the ginger, garlic, onion and the deseeded green chilli in a food processor or blender and blitz for 30 seconds to a thick paste. Set aside.

Heat the oil in a heavy-based shallow pan over a medium heat and add the whole spices including the curry leaves (if using). Fry for 20–30 seconds then add the onion paste. Fry for a further 5–7 minutes or until the mixture is soft and caramel coloured.

Remove from the heat momentarily and add the ground spices, coconut milk, 100 ml (3½ fl oz) water, the whole green chilli and seasoning.

Return to a low heat, stirring frequently, before adding the tomatoes then cook for a further 2–3 minutes.

Gently slide the fish into the sauce in the pan. Cover and simmer to cook through for 6–8 minutes.

Add the remaining lemon juice and the fresh coriander to the sauce before serving.

Serve with Lightly Spiced Spinach (page 115) and Lemon Rice (page 121).

This delicious dish brings back memories for us of family holidays in Kerala.

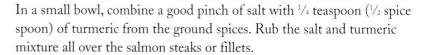

Macchli Kari

Pan-fried Salmon Steaks in a Tomato Sauce

400 g (14 oz) salmon steaks or fillets

2 tablespoons lemon juice

3 tablespoons oil, plus extra for shallow frying

3 cm (1¼ inch) piece of ginger, finely chopped

2 garlic cloves, crushed

1½ tablespoons tomato purée

2 tomatoes, peeled and finely chopped

1 green chilli, split lengthways and deseeded (optional)

Salt and freshly ground black pepper

SERVES 4

FROM YOUR SPICE BOX

WHOLE SPICES

¼ teaspoon (½ spice spoon) cumin seeds

GROUND SPICES

1 teaspoon (2 spice spoons) turmeric

1¼ teaspoons (2½ spice spoons) chilli

½ teaspoon (1 spice spoon) coriander

1 teaspoon (2 spice spoons) fennel

1 teaspoon (2 spice spoons) ginger

In a small bowl, combine a good pinch of salt with ¼ teaspoon (½ spice spoon) of turmeric from the ground spices. Rub the salt and turmeric mixture all over the salmon steaks or fillets.

Drizzle the salmon with 1 tablespoon of the lemon juice and set aside for 30 minutes.

Rinse the salmon under a gentle stream of cold water (this will further remove any fish odours) and drain well before drying between sheets of kitchen paper.

Shallow fry the salmon in a pan of oil, in batches of two until golden, and place on a plate without stacking.

Heat the 3 tablespoons oil in a large heavy-based shallow pan over a medium heat. Add the whole spice and fry until the seeds begin to sizzle. Add the ginger and garlic and fry for 30 seconds.

Reduce the heat and stir in 4 tablespoons water, the remaining turmeric and all the remaining ground spices. Add the tomato purée, tomatoes and a pinch of salt. Stir to keep the mixture in motion so that it does not settle and stick to the saucepan.

When the oil begins to separate from the mixture, pour in 600 ml (1 pint) water and bring to the boil. Gently place the salmon into the sauce. Cover and simmer for 20 minutes.

Reduce the sauce to less than half its initial volume and add the remaining lemon juice, the green chilli (if using) and a pinch of black pepper. Simmer for 1 minute and leave to rest for 10–15 minutes.

Serve with Basmati Rice (page 120) and Courgettes with Green Peppers (page 97).

We finally managed to get this recipe out of Mum!

Macchli Sabe Aur Shimla Mirch

Black Halibut with Apple and Peppers

500 g (1 lb) black halibut fillets (or black-skinned haddock fillets), cut into chunky pieces
1 tablespoon lemon juice
2 tablespoons oil, plus extra for shallow frying
3 eating apples, each cut into quarters
200 g (7 oz) mixed peppers, cored, deseeded and cut into cubes
2 tablespoons tomato purée
Salt
Plain flour, for dusting

To finish
Fresh coriander, chopped
2 tablespoons finely chopped red onion

SERVES 4

FROM YOUR SPICE BOX
WHOLE SPICES
½ teaspoon (1 spice spoon) mustard seeds
½ teaspoon (1 spice spoon) cumin seeds
2 cloves, ground

GROUND SPICES
1½ teaspoons (3 spice spoons) turmeric
¾ teaspoon (1½ spice spoons) chilli
¾ teaspoon (1½ spice spoons) ginger
A good pinch of cumin
½ teaspoon (1 spice spoon) coriander
¾ teaspoon (1½ spice spoons) fennel

Place the fish pieces in a colander. Sprinkle with salt and squeeze over the lemon juice. Rub in 1 teaspoon (2 spice spoons) of turmeric and ¼ teaspoon (½ spice spoon) of ginger from the ground spices, and set aside for 15 minutes.

Wash the fish under a gentle stream of water and dry between sheets of kitchen paper. Then dust each piece lightly with a little plain flour, shaking off any excess.

Heat the oil in a frying pan over a medium heat and fry the fish (skin side down first) in batches until golden brown. Remove with a slotted spoon and leave to one side. Once cool, you can peel the skin away if you wish.

Fry the apple quarters until golden brown in the same oil. Remove with a slotted spoon and leave to one side. Add the mixed peppers to the pan and fry until browned on the edges. Remove with a slotted spoon and leave to one side.

Heat some more oil in a heavy-based saucepan over a medium heat and add the whole spices. When the seeds begin to sizzle add the tomato purée. Reduce the heat and add 200 ml (7 fl oz) water and the remaining ground spices.

Stir and cook for 5 minutes or until the oil separates from the spices and you should have a thick smooth mixture. Add 750 ml (1¼ pints) water and mix well.

Slide the fish into the sauce and cook, covered, for 15 minutes, or until half the sauce remains. Add the apple and peppers and cook for a further 1 minute. Finish with chopped coriander and a little diced onion.

Serve with plain Basmati Rice (page 120).

Sabziyan

Vegetable Dishes

Adraki Zeera Broccoli

Broccoli with Cumin and Ginger

3 tablespoons oil
1 small garlic clove, crushed
1 head of broccoli, cut into
   florets
2 red chillies, halved and
   deseeded
Salt

SERVES 4

FROM YOUR SPICE BOX
WHOLE SPICES
½ teaspoon (1 spice spoon)
   cumin seeds

GROUND SPICES
¼ teaspoon (½ spice spoon)
   ginger

Heat the oil in a heavy-based saucepan over a medium heat and add the whole spice and the garlic. Fry for 30 seconds or until lightly browned.

Remove from heat momentarily then add the broccoli and some salt. Return to the heat and stir-fry for 2 minutes.

Add 400 ml (14 fl oz) water and the ground spice. Cook for a further 5–8 minutes, or until the broccoli is tender. Mix in the chillies and cook for a further minute.

Serve with Red Kidney Beans in a Rich Sauce (page 127), Lamb Rogan Josh (page 64) and Cucumber and Tomato Raita (page 151).

Alexa's children love this 'different' way to serve broccoli.

Bundh Gobhi

Indian Stir-fried Cabbage

3 tablespoons oil

500 g (1 lb) white cabbage, finely shredded

½ teaspoon salt (or to taste)

2–3 red chillies, deseeded and finely sliced

SERVES 6

FROM YOUR SPICE BOX

WHOLE SPICES

½ teaspoon (1 spice spoon) cumin seeds

1 teaspoon (2 spice spoons) mustard seeds

GROUND SPICES

½ teaspoon (1 spice spoon) coriander

½ teaspoon (1 spice spoon) cumin

½ teaspoon (1 spice spoon) ginger

1½ teaspoons (3 spice spoons) turmeric

Heat the oil in a large shallow pan over a medium heat and add the whole spices. When the seeds begin to sizzle, add the cabbage and stir-fry for 1 minute.

Add the salt, fresh red chillies and all of the ground spices. Stir-fry for 8–10 minutes. Cover and cook for 3–4 minutes or until the cabbage is soft and translucent.

Serve with Chicken Rogan Josh (page 46), Roasted New Potatoes with Sesame Seeds (page 94), Spinach with Paneer (page 116) and Tomato Rice (page 124).

This dish is simple to make – whenever we have dinner parties our friends always ask us to cook it.

Simsim Aloo

Roasted New Potatoes with Sesame Seeds

1 kg (2 lb) new potatoes

2 garlic cloves, crushed

3 cm (1¼ inch) piece of ginger, grated

½ small green chilli, deseeded and chopped

3 tablespoons natural yogurt

4 tablespoons finely chopped fresh coriander

2 teaspoons lemon juice

1 tablespoon butter

Salt and freshly ground black pepper

Sesame seeds, for sprinkling

Melted butter, for basting

SERVES 6

FROM YOUR SPICE BOX

WHOLE SPICES

½ teaspoon (1 spice spoon) cumin seeds

GROUND SPICES

¼ teaspoon (½ spice spoon) ginger

¼ teaspoon (½ spice spoon) fennel

½ teaspoon (1 spice spoon) coriander

¼ teaspoon (½ spice spoon) cumin

½ teaspoon (1 spice spoon) chilli

Boil the potatoes in their skins until fork soft. Drain and leave to cool.

In a large bowl mix all of the ingredients with the whole spice and the ground spices. Add the potatoes to the bowl, and leave to marinate for at least 2 hours.

Preheat the oven to 180°C/350°F/Gas mark 4.

Take each potato and place on a baking tray. Sprinkle with the sesame seeds and bake in the preheated oven, on the top shelf, until golden, about 35–40 minutes. Halfway through cooking baste with the melted butter.

Serve with Pan-fried Fruity Aubergine (page 103), Spicy Okra (page 117) and Mushroom Rice (page 126).

These are a great alternative to ordinary roast potatoes. However, they are just as delicious cold and make a good picnic dish.

Tamatar Baigan
Aubergines in Tomato Sauce

1 large aubergine, stem
  removed
2 tablespoons oil, plus extra for
  shallow frying
600 g (1¼ lb) tinned chopped
  tomatoes
Salt
Fresh coriander leaves, to
  finish

SERVES 4

FROM YOUR SPICE BOX

WHOLE SPICES

½ teaspoon (1 spice spoon)
  cumin seeds

GROUND SPICES

1 teaspoon (2 spice spoons)
  chilli
½ teaspoon (1 spice spoon)
  coriander
1 teaspoon (2 spice spoons)
  ginger
1 teaspoon (2 spice spoons)
  turmeric

Cut the aubergine in half lengthways and then across. Take one quarter with the skin facing upwards and cut lengthways into slices 1 cm (½ inch) wide. Do the same for the other quarters.

Sprinkle with a little salt and set aside for 10 minutes as this helps to remove any bitterness naturally present in the aubergine. Rinse away the salt from the aubergine and pat dry between sheets of kitchen paper.

Shallow-fry the slices in batches over a medium heat, taking care to maintain their shape while turning. Remove with a slotted spoon when golden.

Heat the oil in a shallow pan and fry the whole spice until the seeds begin to sizzle. Remove from the heat momentarily and add the ground spices followed by the tomatoes and salt.

Return to the heat and cook for 5–6 minutes stirring frequently until the sauce is thick and reduced.

Arrange the aubergine pieces on top of the sauce at various places in the pan and gradually pour in 100 ml (3½ fl oz) water. Cover and simmer over a low heat for 25–30 minutes, moving the pieces gently and adding more water as the sauce thickens.

If you wish to make the sauce thinner add 50–100 ml (2–3½ fl oz) water and bring to the boil.

Finish with fresh coriander and serve with Tomato Rice (page 124), Paneer with Peas (page 112) and Chicken Tikka (page 44).

Tori aur Shimla Mirch

Courgettes with Green Peppers

300 g (10 oz) courgettes
1 small green pepper
2 tablespoons natural yogurt
2 tablespoons oil
½ tablespoon lemon juice
Salt and freshly ground black
  pepper

SERVES 6

FROM YOUR SPICE BOX

WHOLE SPICES
½ teaspoon (1 spice spoon)
  cumin seeds

GROUND SPICES
1½ teaspoons (3 spice spoons)
  coriander
½ teaspoon (1 spice spoon)
  chilli

Cut one courgette in half lengthways and then across. Take one quarter with the skin facing upwards and cut lengthways into slices 1 cm (½ inch) wide. Do the same for the other quarters.

Cut the green pepper in half, starting from the stem, de-seed and then cut into thin slices of 1 cm (½ inch) thickness.

Mix the yogurt and a pinch of salt with the coriander from the ground spices. Set aside.

Heat the oil in a shallow pan over a medium heat and add the whole spice. When the seeds begin to sizzle, add the courgettes and green pepper and fry for 4 minutes stirring frequently.

Reduce the heat to a minimum and pour in the yogurt mixture. Stir continuously for 3 minutes. Remove from the heat and drizzle with the lemon juice.

To finish, combine a pinch of black pepper with the chilli powder from the ground spices and sprinkle over the dish generously.

Serve with Spiced Mixed Vegetables (page 110), Creamy Paneer (page 114) and your choice of rice and chutney.

Aloo Matar

Potatoes with Peas

75 g (3 oz) frozen peas

3 tablespoons oil

500 g (1 lb) potatoes, peeled and cut into 2 cm (³⁄₄ inch) cubes

1 small onion, finely chopped

¹⁄₂ teaspoon salt (or to taste)

1 tablespoon tomato purée

2 tomatoes, peeled and chopped

1 whole green chilli

2 tablespoons finely chopped fresh coriander

To finish

2 teaspoons butter (optional)

Fresh coriander leaves

SERVES 4

FROM YOUR SPICE BOX

WHOLE SPICES

¹⁄₂ teaspoon (1 spice spoon) cumin seeds

GROUND SPICES

¹⁄₂ teaspoon (1 spice spoon) chilli

¹⁄₂ teaspoon (1 spice spoon) coriander

¹⁄₂ teaspoon (1 spice spoon) cumin

³⁄₄ teaspoon (1¹⁄₂ spice spoons) fennel

¹⁄₂ teaspoon (1 spice spoon) ginger

¹⁄₂ teaspoon (1 spice spoon) turmeric

Boil the peas in water for 5 minutes, drain and refresh in cold water. Set aside.

Heat the oil in a heavy-based saucepan over a medium heat and add the whole spice. When the seeds begin to sizzle, add the potatoes and onion. Fry for 5–6 minutes or until the potatoes turn golden.

Reduce the heat to cool the oil. Add the ground spices, salt, tomato purée, tomatoes and green chilli. Mix well for 1 minute before pouring in 475 ml (16 fl oz) water. Cover and cook for 7 minutes or until the potatoes are tender.

Add the peas and fresh coriander and boil for 1–2 minutes. Dot with butter (if using) and garnish with fresh coriander leaves before serving.

Serve with Spinach with Paneer (page 116), Saffron Rice (page 122) and Mint and Yogurt Chutney (page 152).

Pudeena Sitaphal

Butternut Squash with Cumin and Mint

2 tablespoons oil

600 g (1¼ lb) butternut squash, peeled and chopped into bite-sized pieces

1 green chilli, deseeded and cut in half

2 tablespoons finely chopped fresh mint leaves or 1 teaspoon dried mint leaves

Salt

SERVES 6

FROM YOUR SPICE BOX

WHOLE SPICES

½ teaspoon (1 spice spoon) cumin seeds

Heat the oil in a heavy-based saucepan over a medium heat and add the whole spice. When the seeds begin to sizzle add the butternut squash and the green chilli and fry for a few minutes.

Add 200 ml (7 fl oz) water and leave to cook for 10–12 minutes or until the squash is soft, stirring occasionally.

Remove the halved chilli before serving, if you wish.

Serve with Spiced Pan-fried Chicken (page 42), Basmati Rice (page 120) and Walnut and Mint Chutney (page 146).

Mum often used to make this in Kashmir on a cold winter's day. Steaming hot butternut squash and fresh garden mint on a plain bed of rice – delicious and simple.

Aloo Gobhi

Potatoes and Cauliflower

4 tablespoons oil

1 cauliflower, cut into florets
and then halved

350 g (12 oz) potatoes, peeled
and cut into 3 cm (1¼ inch)
cubes

2.5 cm (1 inch) piece of ginger,
grated

1 tomato, peeled and finely
chopped

1 green chilli, deseeded and
split lengthways

1 tablespoon butter

Salt and freshly ground black
pepper

Fresh coriander leaves, finely
chopped, to finish

SERVES 4

FROM YOUR SPICE BOX

WHOLE SPICES

½ teaspoon (1 spice spoon)
cumin seeds

GROUND SPICES

½ teaspoon (1 spice spoon)
coriander

½ teaspoon (1 spice spoon)
cumin

1 teaspoon (2 spice spoons)
fennel

½ teaspoon (1 spice spoon)
ginger

¾ teaspoon (1½ spice spoons)
turmeric

¼ teaspoon (½ spice spoon)
garam masala

Heat the oil in a shallow pan over a medium heat and fry the whole spice until the seeds begin to sizzle. Add the cauliflower, potatoes, ginger and a pinch of salt. Fry for 5 minutes.

Cover and cook the vegetables for a further 5 minutes, stirring occasionally. If the mixture begins to stick to the bottom of the pan, add 4–5 tablespoons of water (or more if required.)

Momentarily remove from the heat. Add all of the ground spices, except the garam masala, and cook for a further 5 minutes before stirring in the tomatoes, green chilli and 175–200 ml (6–7 fl oz) water.

Cover and simmer for 15 minutes or until the vegetables are tender and the sauce begins to thicken.

Mix the butter, a pinch of pepper and the garam masala from the ground spices into the sauce. Garnish with fresh coriander leaves.

Serve with Lemon Rice (page 121), Spinach and Chickpeas (page 132), Lamb Rogan Josh (page 64) and Coriander Chutney (page 145).

This is Sereena's favourite vegetable dish – she always has a cauliflower in the fridge as Aloo Gobhi is so quick to cook and goes well with any dish.

Dum Aloo

Kashmiri Potatoes

500 g (1 lb) new baby potatoes
2 tablespoons oil, plus extra for deep frying
2 tablespoons natural yogurt
1 tablespoon tomato purée
½ teaspoon salt (or to taste)
1 cm (½ inch) piece of ginger, roughly chopped
2 garlic cloves, roughly chopped

To finish
1 tablespoon butter
A few twists of freshly ground black pepper

SERVES 4

FROM YOUR SPICE BOX
WHOLE SPICES
2 bay leaves
2 cardamom pods, crushed
½ teaspoon (1 spice spoon) cumin seeds
2 cloves
5 cm (2 inch) cinnamon stick

GROUND SPICES
1 teaspoon (2 spice spoons) chilli
½ teaspoon (1 spice spoon) coriander
¼ teaspoon (½ spice spoon) cumin
1 teaspoon (2 spice spoons) fennel
¾ teaspoon (1½ spice spoons) ginger
¼ teaspoon (½ spice spoon) garam masala

Scrub the potatoes in their skins and cover them with lightly salted water in a deep saucepan. Partially cover with a lid and boil until the potatoes are soft on the outer surface but firm in the centre (use a cocktail stick to check the tenderness from time to time). Remove from the heat and run under cold water to cool.

Peel, then prick the potatoes all over with a cocktail stick and deep fry in a heavy-based saucepan over a medium heat until golden. Set aside.

Whisk together the yogurt, 4 tablespoons water, the tomato purée, salt and all the ground spices, except the garam masala. Set aside.

Put the ginger and garlic in a food processor or blender and blitz to a smooth paste, or use a pestle and mortar. Set aside.

Heat the oil in a heavy-based shallow pan over a low heat and add the whole spices. Fry for 30 seconds before adding the ginger–garlic paste then fry for a further 30 seconds.

Add the yogurt mixture and stir frequently for about 8–10 minutes or until the oil separates from the mixture. Pour in 700 ml (24 fl oz) water and add the potatoes.

Combine well by gently stirring and making sure that the sauce does not stick to the bottom of the pan. Cover and cook for 30 minutes over a medium heat, rotating the potatoes occasionally.

Simmer for a further 20 minutes to form a fairly runny sauce that covers the potatoes. Mix the garam masala into the sauce. Before serving, dot with butter and a few twists of black pepper.

Serve with Courgettes with Green Peppers (page 97), Basmati or Lemon Rice (see pages 120 and 121) and Lightly Spiced Spinach (page 115).

Baingan Aloo Aur Sabe Ki Sabzi

Pan-fried Fruity Aubergine

1 aubergine

1 tablespoon oil, plus extra for shallow frying

3 potatoes, each cut into 4 wedges

2 crisp eating apples, each cut into 8 pieces

8 baby plum tomatoes, cut in half

2 tablespoons tomato purée

3 teaspoons lemon juice

2–3 tablespoons finely chopped fresh coriander

Salt

SERVES 4

FROM YOUR SPICE BOX

WHOLE SPICES

1 clove, ground

$\frac{1}{2}$ teaspoon (1 spice spoon) cumin seeds

GROUND SPICES

$\frac{1}{2}$ teaspoon (1 spice spoon) fennel

$\frac{1}{2}$ teaspoon (1 spice spoon) ginger

1 teaspoon (2 spice spoons) turmeric

$\frac{1}{4}$ teaspoon ($\frac{1}{2}$ spice spoon) cumin

$\frac{1}{2}$ teaspoon (1 spice spoon) coriander

1 teaspoon (2 spice spoons) chilli

Cut the aubergine in half lengthways and then across into slices 2 cm ($\frac{3}{4}$ inch) wide. Sprinkle with a little salt and set aside for 10 minutes as this helps to remove any bitterness naturally present in the aubergine. Rinse away the salt from the aubergine and pat dry between sheets of kitchen paper.

Shallow fry the potatoes in a heavy-based frying pan over a medium heat until golden brown. Remove with a slotted spoon and leave to one side. Add the apples to the pan and, turning once, fry for 2 minutes or until lightly browned. Remove with a slotted spoon and leave to one side.

Fry the aubergines in batches, taking care to maintain their shape while turning. Remove with a slotted spoon when browned. Fry the tomatoes for 4–5 minutes or until they are just sealed and lightly browned, making sure they stay whole. Remove with a slotted spoon and leave to one side.

Heat the 1 tablespoon oil in a heavy-based saucepan over a medium heat and add the whole spices. When the seeds begin to sizzle remove from the heat momentarily and add 100 ml ($3\frac{1}{2}$ fl oz) water, some salt and the ground spices. Cook for a few minutes before adding the tomato purée. Stir constantly for 2 minutes until you have a thick paste.

Add the potatoes and another 450 ml ($\frac{3}{4}$ pint) water. Stir, cover and cook for 5 minutes or until the potatoes are just soft. Add 400 ml (14 fl oz) water, lemon juice and the aubergines and apples – make sure the water covers all the vegetables. Cook for 2 minutes and then add the tomatoes. Stir in the fresh coriander before serving.

Serve with Spiced Pan-fried Chicken (page 42) and Cucumber and Tomato Raita (page 151).

Aloo Zeera

Cumin Potatoes

3 tablespoons oil

600 g (1¼ lb) potatoes, peeled and cut into 3 cm (1¼ inch) cubes

¼ teaspoon salt (or to taste)

2 green chillies, sliced lengthways (optional)

2 teaspoons lemon juice

To finish

Fresh coriander, chopped

SERVES 4

FROM YOUR SPICE BOX

WHOLE SPICES

½ teaspoon (1 spice spoon) mustard seeds

½ teaspoon (1 spice spoon) cumin seeds

GROUND SPICES

1 teaspoon (2 spice spoons) coriander

½ teaspoon (1 spice spoon) cumin

½ teaspoon (1 spice spoon) ginger

1 teaspoon (2 spice spoons) turmeric

Heat the oil in a heavy-based shallow pan over a medium heat and add the whole spices. When the seeds begin to sizzle add the potatoes and fry for 12 minutes or until they are golden.

Add the ground spices, salt and fresh green chillies (if using) and continue to fry for a further 3 minutes.

Stir in the lemon juice and 75 ml (3 fl oz) water. Lower the heat and cover for 6 minutes or until the potatoes are tender.

Garnish with fresh coriander and serve as an accompaniment to a main meal or as a starter with Cucumber and Tomato Raita (page 151).

This dish is so versatile as it goes with everything. Our children often ask us to make it for them.

Hari Rajmah

Green Beans

3 tablespoons oil

1 onion, finely sliced

2 cm (³/₄ inch) piece of ginger, grated

3 garlic cloves, crushed

¹/₂ teaspoon salt (or to taste)

400 g (14 oz) green beans, trimmed and cut in half

2 tomatoes, peeled and chopped

1 tablespoon desiccated or flaked coconut (optional)

SERVES 4

FROM YOUR SPICE BOX

WHOLE SPICES

¹/₂ teaspoon (1 spice spoon) cumin seeds

¹/₂ teaspoon (1 spice spoon) mustard seeds

GROUND SPICES

³/₄ teaspoon (1¹/₂ spice spoons) chilli

1 teaspoon (2 spice spoons) ginger

1 teaspoon (2 spice spoons) turmeric

Heat the oil in a shallow pan over a medium heat and add the whole spices. When the seeds begin to sizzle, add the onion, ginger and garlic. Fry for 5 minutes or until the onion is soft and translucent.

Remove from the heat momentarily before adding the ground spices and salt; mix well for 1 minute.

Add 200 ml (7 fl oz) water and the green beans. Cover and cook over a low heat. Stir occasionally for 10 minutes or until soft and tender.

Add the tomatoes and simmer for 10–15 minutes, stirring frequently, to thicken and reduce the sauce until it is fairly dry.

Sprinkle with the coconut (if using) and serve with Potato with Pomegranate (page 30), Monkfish in Coconut Milk (page 86) and Walnut and Mint Chutney (page 146).

Baigan Ka Bhurta
Roasted Aubergine with Tomatoes and Ginger

1 large aubergine
3 tablespoons oil
2 cm (¾ inch) piece of ginger, grated
3 garlic cloves, crushed
1 onion, finely chopped
200 g (7 oz) vine tomatoes, peeled and chopped
2 teaspoons lemon juice
Salt

To finish
Fresh coriander, chopped

SERVES 4

FROM YOUR SPICE BOX
WHOLE SPICES
½ teaspoon (1 spice spoon) cumin seeds

GROUND SPICES
¼ teaspoon (½ spice spoon) ginger
1 teaspoon (2 spice spoons) coriander
¼ teaspoon (½ spice spoon) cumin
½ teaspoon (1 spice spoon) chilli
½ teaspoon (1 spice spoon) fennel
½ teaspoon (1 spice spoon) gram masala

Preheat the oven to 200°C/400°F/Gas mark 6.

Roast the aubergine in the preheated oven for 20–25 minutes or until soft and almost falling apart. Plunge the aubergine into cold water (or ice water) and peel away the skin.

In a bowl, break up the aubergine pulp by mashing with the back of a spoon. Leave to one side.

Heat the oil in a heavy-based saucepan over a medium heat and add the whole spice. When the seeds begin to sizzle add the ginger and garlic and fry for 20–30 seconds.

Add the onion and fry for a further 2–3 minutes, or until the mixture is light brown in colour.

Add the aubergine pulp, ground spices and a pinch of salt. Fry for a further 2–3 minutes. Add the tomatoes and cook for 5–7 minutes.

Lastly, stir in the lemon juice and finish with fresh coriander leaves.

Serve with Potatoes and Cauliflower (page 100), Savoury Rice Flour Pancakes (page 34) and/or Naan bread (see page 138) and Chapatis (see page 139).

Priya recommends this as a great dish for lunch or a light supper.

Bhuna Gucchi

Sautéed Mushrooms

40 g (1½ oz) unsalted butter

3 cm (1¼ inch) piece of root ginger, grated

500 g (1 lb) closed cup mushrooms, halved

1 whole green chilli

2 teaspoons lemon juice

1 tablespoon finely chopped fresh coriander

Salt and freshly ground black pepper

SERVES 4

FROM YOUR SPICE BOX

WHOLE SPICE

½ teaspoon (1 spice spoon) cumin seeds

GROUND SPICES

½ teaspoon (1 spice spoon) chilli

½ teaspoon (1 spice spoon) ginger

Heat the butter in a shallow pan over a medium heat and add the whole spice.

When the seeds begin to sizzle, add the ginger and fry for 15 seconds. Tip in the mushrooms and a pinch of salt. Stir-fry for 30 seconds.

Cover and cook for 10 minutes stirring occasionally. Remove the cover and continue to cook over a low heat for a further 5–7 minutes with occasional stirring.

Continue cooking until the 'sauce' is fairly dry and remove from the heat. Add the green chilli, lemon juice, fresh coriander, a pinch of black pepper and the ground spices.

Return to a low heat and coat the mushrooms well with the ingredients for 1–2 minutes. Serve with Black Chickpeas and Potatoes (page 130), Tomato Rice (page 124) and Salmon in a Tomato Sauce (page 87).

We used to spend hours picking mushrooms in The Valley of Kashmir. Our hand-picked mushrooms tasted delicious.

Aloo Bhindi

Potatoes with Okra

400 g (14 oz) okra
4 tablespoons oil
3 potatoes, cubed
2 teaspoons lemon juice
1 tablespoon finely chopped
   fresh coriander
Salt

SERVES 4

FROM YOUR SPICE BOX
WHOLE SPICES
½ teaspoon (1 spice spoon)
   cumin seeds

GROUND SPICES
½ teaspoon (1 spice spoon)
   chilli
½ teaspoon (1 spice spoon)
   ginger
¼ teaspoon (½ spice spoon)
   cumin
½ teaspoon (1 spice spoon)
   coriander

Wash the okra and dry between sheets of kitchen paper to remove any excess moisture. Top and tail them before cutting each okra into 4–5 pieces.

Heat the oil in a shallow pan or frying pan over a medium heat. When hot add the whole spice and when the seeds start to sizzle add the potatoes.

Fry the potatoes for 2 minutes then add the okra. Stir, cover and cook, stirring occasionally for 15 minutes or until the potatoes are just soft.

Mix in the ground spices and a pinch of salt and cook for a further 5 minutes. Add the lemon juice and fresh coriander and partially cover, if not serving straight away.

Serve with Creamy Paneer (page 114), Lemon Rice (page 121) and/or Naan bread (page 138) and Chapatis (see page 139).

Milli-Julli Sabziyan

Spiced Mixed Vegetables

4 tablespoons oil

2 cm (³/₄ inch) piece of ginger, grated

3 garlic cloves, crushed

1 onion, sliced

100 g (3½ oz) green beans

100 g (3½ oz) baby sweetcorn

1 courgette, cut into 1 cm (½ inch) slices

2 small carrots, cut in half lengthways and sliced

160 g (5½ oz) mixed peppers, deseeded and cut into bite-sized pieces

160 g (5½ oz) cauliflower, cut into small florets

100 g (3½ oz) frozen baby broad beans

1 tablespoon butter

8 baby vine tomatoes, cut in half

1 green chilli, deseeded and sliced lengthways into 4

Salt

To finish

1 teaspoon lemon juice

Fresh coriander, finely chopped (optional)

Spring onions, finely chopped

SERVES 6

FROM YOUR SPICE BOX

WHOLE SPICES

½ teaspoon (1 spice spoon) cumin seeds

½ teaspoon (1 spice spoon) mustard seeds

GROUND SPICES

½ teaspoon (1 spice spoon) ginger

½ teaspoon (1 spice spoon) turmeric

½ teaspoon (1 spice spoon) chilli

1 teaspoon (2 spice spoons) coriander

¼ teaspoon (½ spice spoon) cumin

Heat the oil in a heavy-based shallow saucepan over a medium heat and add the whole spices, followed by the ginger and garlic.

Stir-fry for 30 seconds then add the onion, the rest of the vegetables (except the tomatoes and chilli) and some salt. Cover and cook for 2–3 minutes, stirring occasionally. Then cook for a further 8–10 minutes until the vegetables are crispy but tender.

Remove from the heat momentarily and add the ground spices. Return to a low heat and cook for 2 minutes, mixing well.

Make a well in the middle of the vegetables and add the butter. Add to this the tomatoes, fresh green chilli and a pinch of salt and cook for 4–5 minutes. Gently mix in with the rest of the vegetables.

Finish with fresh coriander, spring onions and a drizzle of lemon juice.

Serve with Butter Chicken (page 43), Basmati Rice (page 120), Kashmiri Potatoes (page 102) and Sweet and Sour Mango Chutney (page 144).

Phoolgobhi Rogan Josh
Dry and Spicy Cauliflower

2 tablespoons Greek yogurt

3 tablespoon ghee or
  2 tablespoons butter and
  1 tablespoon oil

2 cm (3/4 inch) piece of ginger,
  left whole

1 medium cauliflower, cut into
  medium-sized florets

Salt

SERVES 4

FROM YOUR SPICE BOX

WHOLE SPICES

2 bay leaves

2 cloves

3/4 teaspoon (1 1/2 spice spoons)
  cumin seeds

2 cardamom pods, finely
  crushed

GROUND SPICES

1/2 teaspoon (1 spice spoon)
  ginger

3/4 teaspoon (1 1/2 spice spoons)
  fennel

1 teaspoon (2 spice spoons)
  chilli

1/4 teaspoon (1/2 spice spoon)
  garam masala

Mix 50 ml (2 fl oz) water and all of the ground spices, except the garam masala, with the yogurt in a bowl and set aside.

Heat the ghee or butter/oil in a shallow pan over a medium heat and add the whole ginger and the whole spices, except the cardamom. Fry for 30 seconds before adding the cauliflower, 100 ml (3 1/2 fl oz) water and salt. Cover and steam for 10 minutes stirring occasionally.

Once the water content has reduced fully and the ghee or butter/oil becomes visible, fry the florets until they look brown and golden.

Over a low heat, pour the yogurt mixture over the cauliflower and gently combine. Cook for 3–4 minutes, or until the yogurt reduces completely.

Gently mix in the crushed cardamom and the garam masala, taking care not to break the florets. Cook for a further 1 minute. If you wish you can remove the ginger before serving.

Serve with Spinach and Chickpeas (page 132) and Saffron Rice (page 122).

Matar Paneer

Paneer with Peas

4 tablespoons oil
200–250 g (7–8 oz) paneer,
  either home-made (see page
  11) or shop-bought, cut into
  1 cm (½ inch) thick slices
4 tablespoons natural yogurt
200 g (7 oz) peas
Salt

To finish
Fresh coriander, chopped

SERVES 4

FROM YOUR SPICE BOX
WHOLE SPICES
3 cm (1¼ inch) cinnamon
  stick
2 bay leaves
2 cloves, ground
2 cardamom pods, crushed

GROUND SPICES
½ teaspoon (1 spice spoon)
  fennel
½ teaspoon (1 spice spoon)
  ginger
½ teaspoon (1 spice spoon)
  coriander
½ teaspoon (1 spice spoon)
  turmeric
½ teaspoon (1 spice spoon)
  garam masala

Heat the oil in a frying pan over a medium heat and fry the paneer pieces in batches of 5–6 until they are a light brown colour all over. Be careful when frying the paneer as the oil sometimes spits out. Remove with a slotted spoon and leave to one side.

Add the whole spices, except the cardamom, to the same pan and fry in the residual oil for 30 seconds.

Remove from the heat momentarily and pour in 250 ml (8 fl oz) water and the ground spices and a pinch of salt. Bring to the boil and when the oil separates from the water, add another 250 ml (8 fl oz) water.

Gently slide the paneer into the saucepan with the water and spices. Cover and cook over a medium heat for 5 minutes.

Whisk the yogurt with 100 ml (3½ fl oz) water and pour into the saucepan with the paneer. Partially cover and cook for 15 minutes or until the sauce thickens.

Steam or boil the peas for 5 minutes or until the peas are ready to eat. Add to the paneer. Cook for a further 2–3 minutes. Finish with chopped coriander and the crushed cardamom.

Serve with Pan-fried Garlic and Chilli Lamb (page 73), Green Beans (page 105) and Basmati Rice (see page 120).

Paneer

Creamy Paneer

2 tablespoons oil, plus extra for shallow frying
225–250 g (7½–8 oz) paneer, either home-made (see page 11) or shop-bought, cut into 1 cm (½ inch) cubes
2 tablespoons single cream
¼ teaspoon salt (or to taste)
2 tablespoons Greek yogurt
2 tablespoons tomato purée
2½ tablespoons sieved tomatoes (passata)
2 whole green chillies
Oil, for shallow frying
Fresh coriander leaves, finely chopped, to finish

SERVES 4

FROM YOUR SPICE BOX

WHOLE SPICES
2 bay leaves
4 cm (1½ inch) cinnamon stick
¼ teaspoon (½ spice spoon) cumin seeds
1 clove
2 cardamom pods, finely crushed

GROUND SPICES
1 teaspoon (2 spice spoons) fennel
¾ teaspoon (1½ spice spoons) ginger
¾ teaspoon (1½ spice spoons) chilli
¼ teaspoon (½ spice spoon) garam masala

Heat some oil in a frying pan over a medium heat and fry the paneer pieces in batches of 5–6 until a light brown colour all over. Be careful when frying the paneer as the oil sometimes spits out. Remove and place in a bowl of lightly salted water. Set aside.

In a large shallow pan heat the 2 tablespoons oil over a low heat and add the whole spices except the cardamom. Fry for 30 seconds before adding 200 ml (7 fl oz) water, the single cream, salt, fennel and ginger from the ground spices. Bring the mixture to the boil, stirring occasionally, for 2 minutes. Remove from the heat and set aside.

In a bowl, whisk together the yogurt, tomato purée, sieved tomatoes, 2 tablespoons water and the chilli from the ground spices to a smooth consistency. Set aside.

Drain the fried paneer and tip into the pan of cream and spice mixture; cook over a medium heat, stirring, but taking care not to fragment the paneer pieces. When the sauce has almost completely reduced, pour the yogurt mixture over the paneer. Stir gently to combine all the ingredients and cook for 3–4 minutes.

Add 100 ml (3½ fl oz) water, the green chillies, cardamom and garam masala before bringing to the boil. Garnish with finely chopped fresh coriander leaves.

Serve with Kashmiri Potatoes (page 102), Lamb Chops Braised in Saffron Milk (page 60), Basmati Rice (page 120) and Spicy Tomato Dip (page 148).

Alexa is incredibly busy, but she still finds time to make her paneer, while Sereena is a bit impatient so she ends up buying hers. Priya falls between the two.

Sukha Palak

Lightly Spiced Spinach

500 g (1 lb) baby spinach
   leaves
2 tablespoons oil
2 tablespoons butter
½ teaspoon salt (or to taste)
1 garlic clove, crushed
1 tablespoon tomato purée
4 tablespoons sieved tomatoes
   (passata)

To finish
1 green chilli, split lengthways

SERVES 4

FROM YOUR SPICE BOX
WHOLE SPICES
½ teaspoon (1 spice spoon)
   cumin seeds

GROUND SPICES
¾ teaspoon (1½ spice spoons)
   chilli
½ teaspoon (1 spice spoon)
   ginger

Thoroughly wash the spinach leaves in a colander. Set aside for a few minutes to drain. Tip the spinach leaves on to a clean kitchen cloth and pat off any excess moisture.

Heat the oil in a shallow pan over a medium heat and add the whole spice. When the seeds begin to sizzle, add the spinach and cook the leaves in their own juices. Stir and mash the leaves with the back of a wooden spoon until the spinach is wilted and fairly dry. Remove and set aside.

In a shallow pan, heat the butter over a medium heat. Momentarily remove from the heat and add the ground spices, salt, garlic, tomato purée and sieved tomatoes. Stir well to combine for 1–2 minutes, or until the butter separates from the tomato mixture. Then add 3–4 tablespoons water.

Add the spinach leaves, stirring occasionally, and cook for 5–7 minutes, adding a few tablespoons of water from time to time if needed. Finish with the fresh green chilli

Serve with Hot and Spicy Chickpeas (page 134) and Basmati Rice (page 120).

Palak Paneer

Spinach with Paneer

225–250 g (7½ –8 oz) paneer, either home-made (see page 11) or shop-bought, cut into 2.5 cm (1 inch) cubes

300 g (10 oz) baby spinach leaves

3 tablespoons oil, plus extra for shallow frying

1 onion, finely chopped

2 tablespoons tomato purée

¼ teaspoon salt

2 tomatoes, peeled and chopped

1 whole green chilli

SERVES 4

FROM YOUR SPICE BOX

WHOLE SPICES

½ teaspoon (1 spice spoon) cumin seeds

GROUND SPICES

¾ teaspoon (1½ spice spoons) chilli

½ teaspoon (1 spice spoon) ginger

½ teaspoon (1 spice spoon) turmeric

Heat some oil in a frying pan over a medium heat and fry the paneer pieces in batches of 5–6 until a light brown colour all over. Be careful when frying the paneer as the oil sometimes spits out.

Remove and place in a large bowl of lightly salted water. Leave for 10–15 minutes before draining the water off.

Boil 150–200 ml (5–7 fl oz) of water in a deep saucepan and wilt the spinach leaves for 5 minutes. Drain through a sieve and collect the strained water for a later use.

Refresh the leaves with cold water. While in the sieve, mash and tease the spinach leaves to break them up. Set aside.

Heat the 3 tablespoons oil in a shallow pan over a medium heat and add the whole spice. When the seeds begin to sizzle, add the onion and fry until golden brown.

Remove from the heat temporarily and add the ground spices, tomato purée and salt. Return to the heat and fry for 2 minutes, combining the onion with the spice mixture before adding the tomatoes and fresh green chilli.

Cook with occasional stirring for an additional 5 minutes to form a thick sauce. Add the spinach leaves and mash against the sides of the pan to break them up further while stirring.

Add the paneer pieces and 150 ml (¼ pint) of the reserved water from the spinach. Cook for 4–5 minutes stirring gently, taking care not to fragment the paneer. Add more of the cooking water if a runny sauce is preferred. Remove the green chilli if you wish, before serving.

Serve with Spiced Mixed Vegetables (page 110), Lemon Rice (page 121), Cucumber and Tomato Raita (page 151) and/or Naan bread (page 138) and Chapatis (page 139).

Bhindi Masala

Spicy Okra

350 g (11½ oz) okra

2 tablespoons oil

1 onion, roughly chopped

2 cm (¾ inch) piece of ginger, chopped

2 garlic cloves, crushed

½ teaspoon salt (or to taste)

8 cherry tomatoes, sliced

1 tablespoon butter

SERVES 4

FROM YOUR SPICE BOX

WHOLE SPICES

½ teaspoon (1 spice spoon) mustard seeds

½ teaspoon (1 spice spoon) cumin seeds

GROUND SPICES

½ teaspoon (1 spice spoon) chilli

½ teaspoon (1 spice spoon) coriander

¼ teaspoon (½ spice spoon) turmeric

¼ teaspoon (½ spice spoon) garam masala

Wash the okra and dry between sheets of kitchen papers to remove the excess moisture. Top and tail them before cutting into 2 cm (¾ inch) pieces.

Heat the oil in a shallow pan over a medium heat and add the whole spices. When the seeds begin to sizzle, add the onion, ginger and garlic and fry for 1 minute.

Tip in the okra, salt and the ground spices, except the garam masala. Stir to coat the okra with the spice mixture for 5 minutes.

Add the cherry tomatoes and continue to cook the okra for a further 10–15 minutes over a low heat, stirring occasionally. Stir in the butter. Mix in the garam masala before serving.

Serve with Black Chickpeas and Potatoes (page 130), Mushroom Rice (page 126) and Chapatis (page 139).

Dal-chawal

Rice, Beans and Lentils

Basmati Chawal

Basmati Rice

250 g (8 oz) basmati rice
2 teaspoons butter
½ teaspoon salt

SERVES 4

Gently wash the rice in a sieve under cold water for a few minutes until the water runs clear.

Put the rice into a heavy-based saucepan with 600 ml (1 pint) water and leave to soak for 15 minutes.

Add the butter and salt and bring to the boil. Partially cover with a lid and cook for approximately 4–6 minutes until the rice grains are 'al dente'. Cover fully and reduce the heat to a minimum for 5 minutes.

Turn off the heat and set aside to rest for 10 minutes before serving. On serving, fluff-up the rice with a fork to separate the grains and place in a serving dish.

We suggest you serve Basmati Rice with any of the chicken, meat, fish or prawn main dishes in this book.

Nimbu Chawal

Lemon Rice

500 g (8 oz) basmati rice

25 g (1 oz) yellow split
  chickpeas (channa dal)

50 g (2 oz) unsalted butter
  or ghee

1 cm (½ inch) piece of ginger,
  peeled and left whole

Juice of 2 lemons

Salt and freshly ground black
  pepper

SERVES 4

FROM YOUR SPICE BOX

WHOLE SPICES

2 bay leaves

2 cardamom pods, crushed

3 cm (1¼ inch) cinnamon stick

2 cloves

½ teaspoon (1 spice spoon)
  cumin seeds

GROUND SPICES

½ teaspoon (1 spice spoon)
  garam masala

½ teaspoon (1 spice spoon)
  turmeric

Gently wash the rice in a sieve under cold water for a few minutes until the water runs clear then soak in a bowl with enough cold water to cover the rice for 30 minutes.

Wash the lentils in the same way then soak for 4 hours in enough hot water to just cover the lentils. Drain the rice and lentils after the specified times. Set aside.

Heat the butter or ghee in a heavy-based saucepan over a medium heat and add the whole spices, followed by the lentils and black pepper to taste.

Fry for 1 minute then add the rice, ginger, lemon juice, salt to taste, the ground spices and 1 litre (1¾ pints) water. Stir gently and bring to the boil for 5–7 minutes. Partially cover and simmer until the rice grains are just tender. Fully cover and reduce the heat to minimum for 10 minutes.

Remove from the heat and leave to rest without lifting the lid for 10–15 minutes before serving. Fluff up the rice with a fork before transferring to a serving dish.

Some of our friends say that they can't taste rice because it's too bland; well, once they've tasted this they're hooked!

Zafrani Chawal

Saffron Rice

250 g (8 oz) basmati rice

25 g (1 oz) unsalted butter

1 teaspoon oil

10 almonds

10 unsalted cashews

2 cm (1 inch) piece of ginger, grated

2 tablespoons natural yogurt

1 teaspoon saffron threads, soaked in 2 tablespoons warm milk

Salt and freshly ground black pepper

SERVES 4

FROM YOUR SPICE BOX

WHOLE SPICES

2 bay leaves

4 cardamom pods, crushed

8 cm (3½ inch) cinnamon stick

½ teaspoon (1 spice spoon) cumin seeds

Gently wash the rice in a sieve under cold water for a few minutes until the water runs clear.

In a bowl soak the rice in 600 ml (1 pint) water with the whole spices, except the cumin seeds, for 30 minutes. Drain the rice and whole spices, reserving the water for later use. Set aside.

Heat 1 teaspoon of the butter with the oil in a frying pan over a medium heat and fry the nuts until golden.

Remove with a slotted spoon and set aside on kitchen paper to drain.

Heat the remaining butter in a heavy-based saucepan over a medium heat and add the cumin seeds from the whole spices. When the seeds begin to sizzle, add the ginger, salt and pepper.

Fry for 20–30 seconds before adding the drained rice and whole spice mixture. Stir in the yogurt and reserved water, then bring to the boil.

Partially cover and simmer for 3–5 minutes or until the rice grains are soft.

Fully cover the saucepan and reduce the heat to minimum for 6–8 minutes. Remove the lid and spread the nuts over the rice.

Drizzle with saffron milk, replace the lid and rest for 15 minutes before serving.

Fluff up the rice with a fork to separate the grains and transfer to a serving dish.

Serve with a complementary chicken or lamb dish (see Lamb and Chicken chapters) and Sweet and Sour Mango Chutney (page 144).

Tamatar Chawal
Tomato Rice

400 g (14 oz) basmati rice
3 tablespoons ghee or
  5½ tablespoons butter
3 garlic cloves, crushed
2 cm (¾ inch) piece of ginger,
  grated
1 onion, finely chopped
200 g (7 oz) tomatoes, peeled
  and chopped
3 vine tomatoes, peeled and
  finely chopped
1 tablespoon finely chopped
  fresh coriander (optional)
Salt and freshly ground black
  pepper

SERVES 4–6

FROM YOUR SPICE BOX
WHOLE SPICES
½ teaspoon (1 spice spoon)
  cumin seeds
3 bay leaves
3 cardamom pods, crushed

GROUND SPICES
½ teaspoon (1 spice spoon)
  chilli

Gently wash the rice in a sieve under cold water for a few minutes until the water runs clear then soak in a bowl with enough cold water cover the rice for 15 minutes.

Heat the ghee or 4 tablespoons of the butter in a heavy-based saucepan over a medium heat. Add the whole spices and fry for 30 seconds. Then add the garlic, ginger and onion and fry until light brown.

Drain the rice and add to the saucepan with the ground spice. Mix and cook for 3–4 minutes over a low heat.

Put the chopped tomatoes in a food processor or blender with 750 ml (1¼ pints) water and blitz together.

Add this mixture to the saucepan, stir and bring to the boil. Cover and simmer for 10 minutes or until the water has been absorbed into the rice.

In a small frying pan heat the remaining butter and add the remaining chopped vine tomatoes and a pinch of salt. Fry for 2 minutes then add this to the rice.

Cook, covered, over a low heat for 10 minutes or until the rice is soft and fluffy. Mix in the fresh coriander (if using). To stop the rice from burning, place the saucepan on a flat frying pan on top of the heat. Remove any whole spices before serving.

Priya lived on this recipe during her university days – it's so easy it can be put together in minutes.

Sabziyoun Ka Pulao
Favourite Mixed Vegetable Rice

250 g (8 oz) basmati rice

25 g (1 oz) unsalted butter

2 tablespoons oil

1 small potato, diced to 5 mm (¼ inch) cubes

1 onion, finely sliced

3 cm (1¼ inch) piece of ginger, grated

2 garlic cloves, crushed

250 g (8 oz) fresh or frozen mixed vegetables

6 cherry tomatoes, cut in half

300 ml (½ pint) vegetable or chicken stock

SERVES 4

FROM YOUR SPICE BOX

WHOLE SPICES

¼ teaspoon (½ spice spoon) cumin seeds

GROUND SPICES

¼ teaspoon (½ spice spoon) cumin

¼ teaspoon (½ spice spoon) coriander

Gently wash the rice in a sieve under cold water for a few minutes until the water runs clear. Transfer to a bowl with enough water to cover the rice and leave to soak for 30 minutes. Bring to the boil for approximately 4–6 minutes until the rice grains are 'al dente'. Drain off the water and set aside.

Heat the butter and oil in a heavy-based saucepan over a medium heat and fry the whole spice for 30 seconds. When the seeds begin to sizzle add the potato, onion, ginger and garlic, sauté until the mixture turns light brown. Add the ground spices and mix well.

Tip in the mixed vegetables and fry, stirring occasionally, for 4 minutes. Add the tomatoes and fry for a further 1–2 minutes.

Tip in the rice and stir gently to combine all the ingredients. Pour in the stock and reduce the heat to a minimum. Cover and cook for 5–7 minutes. Remove from the heat and serve immediately.

Note: when adding the rice you can also add cooked chicken or prawns to the vegetables to provide an easy, complete meal.

Alexa finds this a great way to get her children to eat vegetables – they love it!

Gucchi Chawal

Mushroom Rice

200 g (7 oz) basmati rice

25 g (1 oz) butter

100 g (4 oz) button
  mushrooms, roughly chopped

1 onion, finely chopped

2 garlic cloves, crushed

375 ml (13 fl oz) vegetable
  stock

To finish

Fresh coriander, roughly
  chopped

Fresh flat leaf parsley, chopped

SERVES 4

FROM YOUR SPICE BOX

WHOLE SPICES

4 cloves

2 bay leaves

1 teaspoon (2 spice spoons)
  cumin seeds

GROUND SPICES

½ teaspoon (1 spice spoon)
  garam masala

Soak the rice in cold water for 10 minutes, then drain and set aside.

Melt half the butter in a heavy-based saucepan over a medium heat and add the spices.

In a separate pan melt the remaining butter, add the mushrooms and fry until golden brown. Remove from the pan and set aside.

Add the onion and garlic to the spices and fry until golden brown. Add the drained rice, cook over a medium heat and stir until it has softened slightly, about 2 minutes.

Add the garam masala and stir. Add the vegetable stock and half of the mushroom mix, then cook the rice over a low heat for 12 minutes with the lid on, until the rice is cooked.

Layer over the rest of the mushroom mixture. Remove the bay leaves, if you wish, before serving and finish with the fresh coriander and parsley.

Rajmah

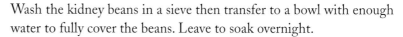

Red Kidney Beans in a Rich Sauce

250 g (8 oz) dried red kidney beans

3 cm (1¼ inch) piece of ginger, roughly chopped

3 garlic cloves, roughly chopped

2 tablespoons oil

1 large onion, finely chopped

1 tablespoon tomato purée

200 g (7 oz) tinned chopped tomatoes

1 small whole green chilli

1 teaspoon butter

3 tablespoons chopped fresh coriander, plus extra to finish

Salt and freshly ground black pepper

SERVES 4

FROM YOUR SPICE BOX

WHOLE SPICES

¼ teaspoon (½ spice spoon) cumin seeds

GROUND SPICES

½ teaspoon (1 spice spoon) chilli

¾ teaspoon (1½ spice spoons) coriander

¼ teaspoon (½ spice spoon) cumin

½ teaspoon (1 spice spoon) garam masala

½ teaspoon (1 spice spoon) ginger

¼ teaspoon (½ spice spoon) turmeric

Wash the kidney beans in a sieve then transfer to a bowl with enough water to fully cover the beans. Leave to soak overnight.

Transfer the beans and their soaking water (adding more water if required) to a saucepan and boil for 1½ hours until the beans are soft. Alternatively, use a pressure cooker following the manufacturer's instructions. Leave to cool.

When cool, drain the beans through a sieve, reserving the liquid. Top up the level of this liquid to 750 ml (1¼ pints) with water. Add the beans and set aside.

Put the ginger and garlic in a food processor or blender and blitz to a smooth paste for 30 seconds (or use a pestle and mortar). Set aside.

Heat the oil in a large heavy-based saucepan over a medium heat and add the whole spice. When the seeds begin to sizzle, add the ginger–garlic paste and fry for 30 seconds. Add the chopped onion reserving 1 tablespoon for the garnish, and sauté until light brown.

Stir in the tomato purée, tomatoes, fresh green chilli, salt, pepper and ground spices. Cook and stir frequently over a low heat for 8–10 minutes, or until a thick sauce develops.

Add the sauce and the kidney beans to a large saucepan and bring to the boil. Simmer over a low heat for 20 minutes, stirring occasionally. If a thicker sauce is desired, heat for a further 10–15 minutes with occasional stirring.

Add the butter and fresh coriander and mix well. Finish with extra coriander leaves and the reserved finely chopped onion. Serve with Basmati Rice (page 120) or Chapatis (page 139).

Gosht ki Biryani
Lamb Biryani

3 cm (1¼ inch) piece of ginger, roughly chopped

3 garlic cloves, roughly chopped

2 green chillies, deseeded and roughly chopped

2 tablespoons roughly chopped fresh coriander

400 ml (14 fl oz) natural yogurt

500 g (1 lb) boneless leg of lamb, cut into cubes

300 g (10 oz) basmati rice

100 g (4 oz) unsalted butter or ghee

1 tablespoon oil

2 onions, finely sliced

½ teaspoon saffron threads, soaked in 4 tablespoons warm milk

Salt

SERVES 4

FROM YOUR SPICE BOX

WHOLE SPICES

2 bay leaves

2 cardamom pods, crushed

5 cm (2 inch) cinnamon stick

GROUND SPICES

½ teaspoon (1 spice spoon) chilli

1 teaspoon (2 spice spoons) cumin

½ teaspoon (1 spice spoon) ginger

½ teaspoon (1 spice spoon) turmeric

1 teaspoon (2 spice spoons) garam masala

To make the marinade, put the ginger, garlic, green chillies, fresh coriander, a pinch of salt, half of the yogurt and the whole and ground spices in a food processor or blender and blitz for 30–40 seconds.

Place the lamb cubes in a bowl and pour the marinade mixture over the meat. Cover and refrigerate overnight.

Gently wash the rice in a sieve under cold water for a few minutes until the water runs clear then soak in 700 ml (24 fl oz) water for 30 minutes. Pour the rice with the water into a saucepan and bring to the boil for 7 minutes. Drain and set aside.

Heat 50 g (2 oz) of the butter and all the oil in a heavy-based saucepan over a medium heat. Add the onions and fry until golden. Remove with a slotted spoon and place on kitchen paper to drain. Set aside.

Add the marinated lamb mixture to the saucepan set over a medium heat. Cover and cook for 15 minutes, stirring occasionally, until the mixture turns fairly dry. Fry the meat pieces for 5–6 minutes until brown.

Transfer the lamb to a bowl. Coat the meat with the remaining yogurt and the fried onions. Set aside. Preheat the oven to 170°C/325°F/Gas mark 3.

Transfer half the meat to a heavy-based ovenproof dish. Layer half of the rice on top and then a second layer of the remaining meat. Finally finish with a layer of the remaining rice. Dot with the remaining butter and drizzle over the saffron milk before sealing firmly with foil.

Cover with a lid and place in the oven for 35 minutes. Remove from the oven and rest for 10 minutes. Before serving, fluff up the rice with a fork and transfer to a serving dish. Serve with Sweet and Sour Mango Chutney (page 144).

Aloo Kale Chaney

Black Chickpeas and Potatoes

2 tablespoons oil

1 onion, finely chopped

3 garlic cloves, crushed

2 cm (³/₄ inch) piece of ginger, grated

400 g (14 oz) tin black chickpeas (or plain chickpeas), rinsed and drained

200 g (7 oz) tinned chopped tomatoes, drained and separated from juice

300 g (10 oz) potatoes, boiled, peeled and chopped into bite-sized pieces

1¹/₂ teaspoons lemon juice

Salt and freshly ground black pepper

To finish

Fresh coriander, chopped

Spring onion, chopped

SERVES 4

FROM YOUR SPICE BOX

WHOLE SPICES

¹/₂ teaspoon (1 spice spoon) cumin seeds

1 teaspoon (2 spice spoons) coriander seeds (optional)

GROUND SPICES

¹/₂ teaspoon (1 spice spoon) chilli

¹/₂ teaspoon (1 spice spoon) turmeric

¹/₄ teaspoon (¹/₂ spice spoon) cumin

¹/₂ teaspoon (1 spice spoon) garam masala

1 teaspoon (2 spice spoon) coriander

Heat the oil in a heavy-based saucepan over a medium heat and add the cumin seeds and coriander seeds (if using).

When the seeds begin to sizzle add the onion, garlic and ginger and fry until golden brown. Add the chickpeas and fry for 2 minutes.

Add the chopped tomatoes, fry for 2–3 minutes. Add 400 ml (14 fl oz) water, the potatoes and lemon juice and bring to the boil. Cook for 4–5 minutes over a medium heat.

Season to taste. Serve sprinkled with fresh coriander and spring onions.

Saboot Masoor Dal
Whole Brown Lentil Dal

250 g (8 oz) whole brown lentils

1.5 litres (2½ pints) hot water

2 teaspoons salt, plus extra for seasoning

3 tablespoons oil

3 garlic cloves, crushed

2 cm (¾ inch) piece of ginger, grated

1 onion, finely chopped

200 g (7 oz) tomatoes, chopped

2 tablespoons lemon juice

1 whole green chilli, pierced

4 tablespoons finely chopped fresh coriander

1 tablespoon butter

SERVES 6

FROM YOUR SPICE BOX

WHOLE SPICES

½ teaspoon (1 spice spoon) cumin seeds

GROUND SPICES

½ teaspoon (1 spice spoon) ginger

½ teaspoon (1 spice spoon) chilli

A good pinch cumin

¾ teaspoon (1½ spice spoons) coriander

½ teaspoon (1 spice spoon) turmeric

Pick over the lentils for any stones. Wash and leave to soak in the hot water overnight with the salt, covered.

Boil the lentils in their soaking water until soft.

Heat the oil in a saucepan over a medium heat. Add the cumin seeds, garlic and ginger and fry until lightly brown. Add the onion and fry until golden brown.

Add the ground spices and salt to taste and stir for 1 minute. Add the tomatoes and cook for 5 minutes or until a thick pulp is formed.

Add this to the lentils and bring to the boil. Partially cover and simmer, stirring occasionally, for 5–8 minutes.

Add the lemon juice, whole green chilli, fresh coriander and butter. Add more water if it is too thick, although this lentil dish should be quite thick in texture.

A very wholesome, nutritious dal made with whole lentils.

Palak Aur Channa

Spinach and Chickpeas

500 g (1 lb) baby spinach
  leaves
3 tablespoons oil
125 g (4 oz) tinned chickpeas
3 vine tomatoes, finely
  chopped
1 whole green chilli, pierced
Salt

SERVES 4

FROM YOUR SPICE BOX

WHOLE SPICES
¾ teaspoon (1½ spice spoons)
  cumin seeds

GROUND SPICES
½ teaspoon (1 spice spoon)
  chilli
½ teaspoon (1 spice spoon)
  ginger

Wash the spinach and leave to drain, squeezing out all of the water with a clean cloth.

Heat 2 tablespoons of the oil in a heavy-based saucepan over a medium heat and add ¼ teaspoon (½ spice spoon) of cumin seeds. When the seeds begin to sizzle add the chickpeas.

Stir-fry for 1 minute then add the ground spices and some salt. Stir for a further 30 seconds and add 100 ml (3½ fl oz) water. Cook for 1 minute and leave to one side.

Heat another saucepan with the remaining oil over a medium heat and add the chopped tomatoes. Fry for 2–3 minutes, remove with a slotted spoon then leave to one side.

Now add the remaining cumin seeds to the saucepan. Add the spinach, stir and break up the leaves with the back of a wooden spoon until it forms a pulp. Cook for 1 minute and add the green chilli. Make sure that some liquid still remains.

Transfer the spinach with any remaining liquid and the tomatoes to the saucepan containing the chickpeas. Mix and cook for 1 minute. Remove the whole chilli, if you wish, before serving.

Serve with Naan bread (page 138) and Lemon Rice (see page 121).

Cholay

Hot and Spicy Chickpeas

250 g (8 oz) dried chickpeas or 400 g (14 oz) tinned chickpeas, drained and rinsed
3 cm (1¼ inch) piece of ginger, grated
3 garlic cloves, crushed
2 tablespoons oil
2 large onions, finely chopped
1½ tablespoons tomato purée
2 whole green chillies
3 teaspoons salt (or to taste)
300 g (10 oz) tinned chopped tomatoes
1 teaspoon butter (optional)
3 tablespoons chopped fresh coriander, plus extra to finish
Freshly ground black pepper

SERVES 6

FROM YOUR SPICE BOX

WHOLE SPICES
¼ teaspoon (½ spice spoon) cumin seeds

GROUND SPICES
1 teaspoon (2 spice spoons) chilli
1 teaspoon (2 spice spoons) coriander
½ teaspoon (1 spice spoon) cumin
1 teaspoon (2 spice spoons) garam masala
½ teaspoon (1 spice spoon) turmeric

If you are using dried chickpeas, wash them in a sieve then transfer to a bowl with enough water to fully cover the chickpeas. Leave to soak overnight.

Boil the chickpeas in a large saucepan adding more water if required until the chickpeas are soft. Alternatively, use a pressure cooker following the manufacturer's instructions. When cool, drain the chickpeas through a sieve, retaining the stock. Measure the stock and top up the liquid to 400 ml (14 fl oz) with water. Add the chickpeas to the water and set aside. If you are using tinned chickpeas simply add 400 ml (14 fl oz) water to them in a large bowl and set aside.

Put the ginger and garlic in a food processor or blender and blitz to a smooth paste for 20–30 seconds, or use a pestle and mortar. Set aside.

Heat the oil in a large heavy-based saucepan over a medium heat and add the whole spice. When the seeds begin to sizzle, add the ginger–garlic paste and fry for 30 seconds. Add the onions (reserving 1 tablespoon to use as a garnish) and sauté until light brown. Remove from the heat momentarily and add the ground spices, tomato purée, green chillies, salt and a few twists of black pepper. Return to the heat and mix well for 30 seconds.

Stir in the chopped tomatoes and cook, stirring frequently, over a low heat for 6–8 minutes, or until a thick sauce develops. Add the chickpeas with the stock to the sauce. Cover and simmer over a low heat for 15–18 minutes stirring occasionally. Reduce for a further 15–18 minutes over a medium heat with occasional stirring if a thicker sauce is desired.

Add the butter (if using) and fresh coriander and mix well into the sauce. Sprinkle with extra coriander and the reserved onion before serving. Serve with Sweet and Sour Mango Chutney (page 144) and Pan-fried Potato Flatbread (page 143).

A wonderful street food that has been enjoyed for centuries.

Masoor Dal

Red Split Lentil Dal

250 g (8 oz) red split lentils
1 large onion, finely chopped
2 large tomatoes, peeled and
  chopped
3 cm (1¼ inch) piece of ginger,
  grated
2 whole green chillies
3 garlic cloves, crushed
1½ tablespoons oil
Salt and freshly ground black
  pepper

To finish
Fresh coriander leaves
2 teaspoons lemon juice

SERVES 4

FROM YOUR SPICE BOX
WHOLE SPICES
½ teaspoon (1 spice spoon)
  cumin seeds
¼ teaspoon (½ spice spoon)
  mustard seeds

GROUND SPICES
1 teaspoon (2 spice spoons)
  coriander
1 teaspoon (2 spice spoons)
  ginger
1½ teaspoons (3 spice spoons)
  turmeric

Wash the lentils for a few minutes in a sieve then transfer to a deep saucepan with 1.2 litres (2 pints) water, a pinch of salt, the onion (reserving 1 tablespoon to use as a garnish), tomatoes, ginger, green chillies, the ground spices and half of the garlic.

Partially cover, bring to the boil and then simmer for 10–15 minutes, or until the lentils are soft and nearly doubled in size. Remove from the heat and set aside.

Heat the oil in a frying pan over a medium heat and add the whole spices. When the seeds begin to sizzle, tip in the remaining garlic and fry for 30 seconds.

Remove from the heat and pour directly over the dal (lentils), which may sizzle at the surface for a few seconds. Mix thoroughly. Finish with fresh coriander leaves, lemon juice, the reserved chopped onion and a twist of black pepper.

Serve hot with Basmati Rice (page 120) or Chapatis (see page 139).

Roti Aur Chutneys

Bread and Chutneys

Naan

Leavened Bread

1 teaspoon sugar

100 ml (3½ fl oz) lukewarm
   water

1 teaspoon dried yeast

250 g (8 oz) plain flour, plus
   extra for dusting

1 teaspoon salt

¼ teaspoon baking powder

2 tablespoons natural yogurt

2 tablespoons oil

2 teaspoons onion seeds
   (optional)

1 tablespoon melted butter, for
   brushing

Pizza stone (optional)

MAKES 6

Mix the sugar with 1–2 teaspoons water in a bowl and add the yeast to activate. Leave in a warm place for 10–15 minutes until the liquid is frothy.

Sift the flour, salt and baking powder together into a large bowl. Make a well in the centre and add the yeast mixture, yogurt and oil.

Combine all of the ingredients by hand to form a soft dough, adding the remaining warm water and more flour, if required. Alternatively, use a food processor with a dough-kneading attachment.

Lightly oil a large bowl and put the dough in the centre. Cover and keep in a warm place for 3–4 hours, or until the dough has doubled in size.

Dust a work surface with flour and punch down the dough and knead for 5 minutes. Sprinkle the onion seeds (if using) on the work surface and roll the dough ball over the seeds. Divide into 6 equal balls and cover with a damp cloth.

Preheat the oven to 200°C/400°F/Gas mark 6. Heat the pizza stone (if using) in the oven until hot

Roll out each dough ball, one at a time, into a 20 cm (8 inch) circle. Wet your palms with water and lift the circle of dough, transferring from one palm to the other a couple of times to form a tear-shaped naan. Place on to the hot pizza stone for 3-4 minutes. As the naan rises, it forms brown flecks evenly over the surface; remove from the oven and brush lightly with melted butter. Stack the baked naans, one on top of the other, and wrap in foil to keep warm.

If you do not have a pizza stone, preheat a grill pan on a high setting and place the naan under the grill for 3-4 minutes on each side, or until the naan has risen and has brown flecks. Brush with melted butter.

Chapati

Wholewheat Flatbread

225 g (7½ oz) fine wholewheat (atta) flour, plus extra for dusting
Pinch of salt
2 tablespoons oil or ghee
75–125 ml (3–4 fl oz) warm water
1 tablespoon melted butter, for brushing (optional)

MAKES ABOUT 10–12

Sift the flour and salt together in a large bowl. Make a well in the centre and pour in the oil or ghee.

Slowly pour the measured water into the well, while using your hand to combine to form a dough ball. Alternatively, use a food processor with a dough-kneading attachment.

Turn out on to a lightly floured board and knead for about 10 minutes into a non-sticky pliable dough. To test, press lightly with your fingertip and if it springs back, it is ready. Cover with a damp cloth and set aside for 30–60 minutes.

Knead the dough once more for about 5 minutes then divide into 10–12 equal balls. Keep covered with a damp cloth, removing one at a time for rolling.

Heat a griddle or a flat non-stick frying pan over a medium heat until hot.

Dust a work surface with flour and roll out a single dough ball into a thin 15 cm (6 inch) circle. Lift it on to one hand and slap it firmly on to the hot griddle.

When the colour changes and the surface begins to form bubbles, flip it over using a spatula to cook on the other side. Pan-bake for 10 seconds then press lightly on the chapati with a clean towel or spoon to encourage it to puff up.

Remove with tongs and brush lightly with melted butter (if using).

Before pan-baking the second chapati, wipe off any charred flour left by the previous one with kitchen paper. Stack the cooked chapatis one on top of the other, and wrap in foil to keep them warm.

We think chapatis are best served hot and are the perfect accompaniment to a variety of Indian meals.

Poori

Deep-fried Bread

300 g (10 oz) plain flour

200 g (7 oz) wholemeal flour
(sifted husks removed)

¼ teaspoon salt

1 tablespoon oil

Oil, for deep frying

MAKES ABOUT 16

FROM YOUR SPICE BOX
WHOLE SPICES

½ teaspoon (1 spice spoon)
cumin seeds

Toast the cumin seeds in a small frying pan until lightly browned then add to a bowl with the rest of the ingredients.

Mix together with just enough lukewarm water to form a stiff dough. Knead well. Alternatively, use a food processor with a dough-kneading attachment. Leave to rest covered with a damp cloth for 30 minutes.

Knead again until you have a non-sticky pliable dough. To test, press lightly with your fingertip and if it springs back, it is ready.

Divide into about 16 small balls the size of an apricot, and roll each out into a circle about 10–12 cm (4–5 inches) wide. Cover with a damp cloth.

Heat the oil in a deep wok-style pan until hot, or until a cube of bread cooks in 30 seconds when dropped in. Take one poori and slide it into the oil. Using a slotted spoon, press lightly on the poori so that it puffs up.

When golden remove and drain on sheets of kitchen paper. Do not pile on one another, as they will deflate.

If you travel around India you will find that food is inexpensive, especially if you eat in dhabbas – they all have clay ovens and toss these piping hot poori on your plate one after another.

Phulka Wrap
Flatbread Wraps

500 g (1 lb) fine wholewheat
    (atta) flour, plus extra for
    dusting
Pinch of salt
350–375 ml (12–13 fl oz)
    warm milk
Oil, ghee or melted butter, for
    brushing

MAKES ABOUT 16

FROM YOUR SPICE BOX
GROUND SPICES
¼ teaspoon (½ spice spoon)
    chilli

Sift the flour, salt and chilli powder together in a large bowl. Slowly pour the milk into the flour, while using your hand to combine to form a dough ball. Alternatively, use a food processor with a dough-kneading attachment.

Turn out on to a lightly floured board and knead for about 10 minutes into a non-sticky pliable dough. To test, press lightly with your fingertip and if it springs back, it is ready. Cover with a damp cloth and set aside for 30–60 minutes. Knead the dough once more for about 5 minutes then divide into 16 equal balls. Keep covered with a damp cloth, removing one dough ball at a time for rolling.

Dust the surface of a board with flour and roll out a single dough ball into a thin 15 cm (6 inch) circle. Brush oil, ghee or melted butter over the surface of the circle and lightly dust with flour.

Set aside while you roll out a second circle to a similar size and then, lay it over the oiled one. Firmly press the two layers together using the palm of your hand. These two sandwiched layers now form two wraps. Roll out the sandwiched circle to about 18 cm (7 inches). Roll out the rest of the dough balls in the same way, keeping them covered under a damp cloth.

Heat a griddle or a flat non-stick frying pan over a medium heat until hot.

Fully extend your fingers and lift the sandwiched layers on to it. Slap it firmly down on to the hot griddle. If you find this difficult roll it up around a rolling pin and unroll on the hot griddle. Turn down the heat to a minimum and pan-bake for 3 minutes, or until the underside of the wrap has brown spots at various points of contact.

Flip it over using a spatula to cook on the other side for 2 minutes while pressing lightly with a clean towel or spoon to encourage the wraps to puff up. Remove from the heat with tongs and pull the two layers apart. Take care while doing this, as trapped hot air between the wraps will escape. Store the cooked phulka wraps in foil and serve hot with your choice of recipe.

Aloo Paratha

Pan-fried Potato Flatbread

225 g (7½ oz) wholewheat (atta) flour, plus extra for dusting

½ teaspoon salt (or to taste)

2 tablespoons oil or ghee

75–125 ml (3–4 fl oz) warm water

250 g (8 oz) potatoes

1 tablespoon lemon juice

1 onion, finely chopped

2 tablespoons finely chopped fresh coriander

1 tablespoon melted butter, for brushing

MAKES ABOUT 10

FROM YOUR SPICE BOX
GROUND SPICES

1 teaspoon (2 spice spoons) chilli

1 teaspoon (2 spice spoons) coriander

1 teaspoon (2 spice spoons) cumin

½ teaspoon (1 spice spoon) garam masala

Sift the flour with a pinch of salt into a large bowl. Make a well in the centre and pour in the oil. Slowly pour the measured water into the well using your hand to combine to form a dough ball. Alternatively, use a food processor with a dough-kneading attachment.

Turn out on to a lightly floured board and knead for about 10 minutes into a non-sticky pliable dough. To test, press lightly with your fingertip and if it springs back, it is ready. Cover with a damp cloth and set aside for 30–60 minutes.

Boil the potatoes in their skins until tender. Drain, cool and peel off the skins. Mash the potatoes with all the ground spices, the lemon juice, onion, fresh coriander and the remaining salt. Mix well.

Knead the dough once more for about 5 minutes then divide and shape into 10 equal balls. Keep covered with a damp cloth, removing one dough ball at a time for rolling.

Roll out a single dough ball into a 15 cm (6 inch) circle. Spread one portion of the mashed potato mixture on half of the circle and fold into a semi-circle.

Brush with melted butter on half of the surface and fold over into a quarter. Dust with flour and roll out evenly to double its size. Repeat for the other dough balls and keep the rolled out parathas covered with a damp cloth.

Heat a griddle or a large flat non-stick frying pan until hot over a medium heat. Gently lift each paratha on to the griddle and allow it to pan-bake for 2 minutes on one side and 1 minute on the other.

Brush with 1–2 teaspoons of melted butter over the entire surface and pan-fry for 30 seconds on one side and then the other. Remove and wrap in foil to keep warm. Serve with Dry and Spicy Cauliflower (page 111).

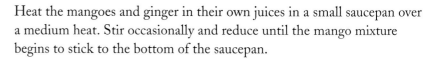

Aam ki Chutney
Sweet and Sour Mango Chutney

250 g (8 oz) green mangoes (unripe), peeled and grated

2.5 cm (1 inch) piece of ginger, grated

50 g (2 oz) sugar

¼ teaspoon salt (or to taste)

1 teaspoon vinegar

SERVES 4–6

FROM YOUR SPICE BOX
GROUND SPICES
½ teaspoon (1 spice spoon) chilli

¼ teaspoon (½ spice spoon) garam masala

Heat the mangoes and ginger in their own juices in a small saucepan over a medium heat. Stir occasionally and reduce until the mango mixture begins to stick to the bottom of the saucepan.

Add the sugar and stir frequently for 8–10 minutes or until the mango mixture begins to have a jam-like consistency.

Add the salt and ground spices and combine well for a further 2 minutes.

Stir in the vinegar and as the mixture loosens, begin to mix constantly for a further 2 minutes.

Cool slightly and while still warm pour into a serving bowl. Serve as an accompaniment with the main meal or with starters. Alternatively, pour into a sterilized jar and when completely cold, seal the jar and store in the fridge for up to 5 days.

To make a larger quantity, increase all of the ingredients four-fold.

Dhania Chutney

Coriander Chutney

2 teaspoons olive oil

60 g (2½ oz) fresh coriander, plus extra to garnish

1 green chilli, deseeded and cut in half

¼ teaspoon salt (or to taste)

3 tablespoons Greek yogurt

SERVES 6

FROM YOUR SPICE BOX

WHOLE SPICES

½ teaspoon (1 spice spoon) mustard seeds

Heat the oil in a small frying pan over a medium–high heat and add the whole spice. When the seeds begin to sizzle, remove from the heat and set aside.

Put the coriander, green chilli, salt and 1 tablespoon of the yogurt in a food processor or blender and blitz to a smooth paste.

Add the oil–spice mixture and the remaining yogurt to the paste and blend for a further 3 seconds.

Garnish with coriander leaves and serve chilled with starters or as an accompaniment to a main meal.

A North Indian favourite with a lot of vitamin zest.

Ahkrot-Pudina Chutney
Walnut and Mint Chutney

10 freshly shelled walnuts or
  40 g (1½ oz) walnut pieces
4 tablespoons chopped fresh
  mint
½ small green chilli, deseeded
  and chopped
6 tablespoons natural yogurt
1 teaspoon lemon juice
2 teaspoons olive oil
Salt, to taste

FROM YOUR SPICE BOX
WHOLE SPICES
Pinch of mustard seeds
Pinch of cumin seeds

If using freshly shelled walnuts, soak them in hot water for 5 minutes or until it is easy to peel away their skins.

Put the walnuts, mint, green chilli, 2 tablespoons of the yogurt, salt and lemon juice in a food processor or blender and blitz to a smooth consistency. Pour into a bowl and mix in the remaining yogurt.

Heat the olive oil in a small frying pan over a medium heat and add the whole spices.

When the seeds are lightly browned add to the bowl with the yogurt. Finish with a few mint leaves. A cooling accompaniment to a main meal.

This is great for those who don't like things too hot and spicy but enjoy the texture of a chutney.

Saeb-Adrak Aur Dalchini Chutney

Apple, Ginger and Cinnamon Chutney

3 eating apples

3 teaspoons dark brown sugar

2 teaspoons lemon juice

4 cm (1½ inch) piece of
ginger, cut into fine strips

A pinch of nutmeg

Salt and freshly ground black
pepper

5–6 fresh mint leaves, finely
chopped, plus extra to finish

SERVES 6

FROM YOUR SPICE BOX
WHOLE SPICES

3 cm (1¼ inch) cinnamon stick

1 cardamom pod, crushed

2 cloves

Wash, peel and core the apples and chop into small cubes.

Heat a small saucepan over a low heat and add the apples, sugar, lemon juice, ginger, whole spices, nutmeg and seasoning.

Cook, stirring occasionally, for 5–6 minutes or until the apple mixture is soft and pulp-like. Add the mint.

Decorate with mint leaves to serve. Store in an airtight container in the fridge.

Tamatar Chutney
Spicy Tomato Dip

400 g (14 oz) ripe tomatoes,
 finely chopped
2 tablespoons olive oil
3 garlic cloves, roughly
 chopped
1 onion, finely chopped
2 green chillies, deseeded and
 finely chopped
¼ teaspoon salt (or to taste)
1 tablespoon sugar
1 tablespoon lemon juice

SERVES 6

FROM YOUR SPICE BOX
WHOLE SPICES
½ teaspoon (1 spice spoon)
 cumin seeds

Heat a small frying pan over a medium heat and dry roast the cumin seeds for 30 seconds until the seeds turn dark brown. When cool, coarsely grind the toasted cumin seeds using a pestle and mortar. Set aside.

Tip the tomatoes into a small saucepan, cover and cook over a medium heat for 4 minutes in their own juice until soft. Set aside.

Heat the oil in a heavy-based saucepan over a medium heat and sauté the garlic and onion for 3 minutes, or until soft and translucent.

Add the green chillies, salt, sugar and lemon juice and stir well to combine. Remove from the heat.

Put the tomatoes, roasted whole spice and the onion mixture in a food processor or blender and blitz to a smooth purée.

Serve this sweet-spicy sauce with starters like Samosas (page 24) and Lamb Kebabs (page 26).

'Some Like It Hot' is what Sereena says whenever she eats this dip.

Bhuna Huva Baigan Raita

Smoked Aubergine Raita

2 aubergines, stems intact
250 ml (8 fl oz) natural yogurt
1 red chilli, deseeded and
  finely sliced
1 shallot, finely chopped
1 garlic clove, finely chopped
Salt and freshly ground black
  pepper
Fresh coriander leaves, finely
  chopped, to finish

SERVES 6

FROM YOUR SPICE BOX
WHOLE SPICES
½ teaspoon (1 spice spoon)
  cumin seeds

Preheat the oven to 200°C/400°/Gas mark 6.

Place both aubergines in the centre of the preheated oven on a roasting tray keeping a small distance between them. Roast for 30–35 minutes or until the outside skin cracks and turns a deep brown-black colour.

Remove the aubergines by their stems and dip into a bowl of cold water. Peel off the skin.

Cut off the stems and put the aubergines in a food processor or blender with the yogurt, red chilli, chopped shallot and garlic. Blend to a smooth consistency and pour the mixture (raita) into a serving dish.

Season with salt and pepper, cover and chill in the fridge for 2 hours.

Heat a small frying pan over a medium heat and dry roast the cumin seeds for 30 seconds until the seeds turn dark brown. When cool, coarsely grind the toasted cumin seeds using a pestle and mortar.

Garnish the raita with the dry roasted spice and fresh coriander leaves.

This creamy yogurt chutney is full of texture and perfect served with starters or as an accompaniment to a main meal.

Aloo Aur Kabooli Channa Raita

Chickpea and Potato Raita

1 teaspoon butter

2 potatoes, boiled, peeled and cubed

1 small onion, finely chopped

400 g (14 oz) Greek yogurt

150 g (5 oz) tinned chickpeas, drained

4 tablespoons finely chopped fresh coriander

1 green chilli, halved lengthways (one half finely chopped, the other set aside for a garnish)

2 tablespoons single cream (optional)

Salt

SERVES 6

FROM YOUR SPICE BOX

WHOLE SPICES

½ teaspoon (1 spice spoon) cumin seeds

A good pinch of mustard seeds

GROUND SPICES

A pinch of chilli

Heat a small frying pan over a medium heat and dry roast the cumin seeds for 30 seconds until the seeds turn dark brown. When cool, coarsely grind the toasted cumin seeds using a pestle and mortar and tip them into a mixing bowl. Set side.

To the same frying pan add the butter and fry the mustard seeds until they pop.

In a bowl mix together all of the remaining ingredients and add half of the mustard seeds and ground cumin seeds. Transfer to a serving bowl. Sprinkle with the remaining ground cumin seeds and mustard seeds and top with a halved green chilli to finish.

Kheera aur Tamatar Raita

Cucumber and Tomato Raita

400 ml (14 fl oz) natural
  yogurt
1 tablespoon finely chopped
  fresh mint leaves, plus extra
  leaves to finish
¼ cucumber, peeled and grated
2 cherry tomatoes, finely
  chopped
Salt and freshly ground black
  pepper

SERVES 4

FROM YOUR SPICE BOX
WHOLE SPICES
¼ teaspoon (½ spice spoon)
  cumin seeds

GROUND SPICES
A pinch of chilli

Heat a small frying pan over a medium heat and dry roast the cumin seeds for 30 seconds until the seeds turn dark brown. When cool, coarsely grind the toasted cumin seeds using a pestle and mortar.

Whisk the yogurt to a smooth consistency in a bowl and add the dry roasted spice, mint leaves, salt and pepper. Set aside.

Gently squeeze out any water from the cucumber in a clean tea towel and separate the grated strands into a serving bowl.

Add the tomatoes and fold in the yogurt mixture. Sprinkle with a pinch of chilli and garnish with fresh mint leaves. Cover and refrigerate until ready to serve. Serve with any spicy meal as it has a wonderful cooling effect.

Priya makes a large bowl of this and eats it as part of her healthy-eating regime – this is the most amazing raita she's ever tasted.

Pudina-Dahi Chutney
Mint and Yogurt Chutney

25 g (1 oz) fresh mint leaves,
  plus extra to garnish
250 g (8 oz) Greek yogurt
½ green chilli, deseeded and
  chopped
Salt

SERVES 4

Put all of the ingredients in a food processor or blender and blitz until smooth. Pour into a serving dish and top with mint leaves.

Serve with Vegetable Fritters (page 22).

Sereena makes this as a side dish for friends who don't like their food too hot and spicy.

Imli Chutney
Tamarind Chutney

300 g (10 oz) tamarind

475 ml (16 fl oz) boiling water

1½ tablespoons light olive oil

¼ teaspoon salt

6 tablespoons dark brown
muscovado sugar

SERVES 4

FROM YOUR SPICE BOX

WHOLE SPICES

½ teaspoon (1 spice spoon)
cumin seeds

GROUND SPICES

½ teaspoon (1 spice spoon)
chilli

Soak the tamarind in the boiling water, breaking the pulp down with the back of a spoon. Leave for about 10–15 minutes.

Sieve the tamarind to remove the pulp and juice. Leave to one side.

Heat a small frying pan over a medium heat and dry roast the cumin seeds for 30 seconds until the seeds turn dark brown. When cool, grind the toasted cumin seeds using a pestle and mortar to a fine powder.

Heat the oil in a heavy-based saucepan over a medium heat and add the ground cumin and chilli powder with all the rest of the ingredients.

Stir well and leave to cook for 6–8 minutes, stirring occasionally. Leave to cool. Store in an airtight container in the fridge for 4–6 days.

Serve with Potato with Pomegranate (page 30).

Mishthaan Aur Sharbat

Desserts and Drinks

Gajar ka Halva
Carrot and Nut Dessert

1 kg (2 lb) carrots, grated
1 litre (1¾ pints) whole milk
15 g (½ oz) flaked almonds
15 g (½ oz) ground almonds
15 g (½ oz) raisins
½ teaspoon ground cinnamon
200 ml (7 fl oz) single cream
100 g (3½ oz) ghee
60 g (2½ oz) granulated sugar
1 teaspoon saffron threads,
  soaked in 3 tablespoons warm
  milk

SERVES 4

FROM YOUR SPICE BOX
WHOLE SPICES
3 cardamom pods, finely
  crushed

To finish
10 g (½ oz) unsalted
  pistachios, finely chopped
Crème fraîche

In a large heavy-based saucepan over a medium heat, place the carrots, milk, nuts, raisins, cinnamon and cardamom from the whole spice. Cook for 30 minutes stirring frequently.

Add the cream and continue stirring over a low heat. Reduce the carrot mixture until there is little or no moisture present.

Stir in the ghee and combine well for 10 minutes. Add the sugar and stir for a further 5 minutes. Remove from the heat and drizzle with saffron milk.

Serve hot in individual bowls topped with chopped pistachios and fresh crème fraîche.

Sereena loves this dessert, it's fragrant, sweet and very comforting in cold weather.

Kheer

Sweet Rice

75 g (3 oz) arborio (risotto) rice
1.2 litres (2 pints) whole milk
40 g (1½ oz) granulated sugar
15 g (½ oz) flaked almonds

To finish
10–12 pieces of flaked almonds
Edible silver leaf (optional)
1 teaspoon saffron threads, soaked in 3 tablespoons warm milk

SERVES 4

FROM YOUR SPICE BOX
WHOLE SPICES
6 cardamom pods, finely crushed

Gently wash the rice in a sieve under cold water for a few minutes until the water runs clear then transfer to a bowl with enough water to cover the rice. Leave to soak for 30 minutes.

Drain and crush the rice with your hand or with the back of a wooden spoon until most of the grains are broken.

Boil the milk and rice in a large heavy-based saucepan over a medium heat. When the milk starts to boil, stir frequently and press with the back of a wooden spoon against the sides of the saucepan to mash the rice grains.

Simmer for 1 hour, stirring frequently, as well as scraping thickened milk from the bottom and sides of the pan to reduce the liquid.

Add the sugar, almonds and crushed cardamoms. Stir regularly for a further 30 minutes or until the rice softens and the milk thickens.

To test whether the rice is ready, place 2 tablespoons on a plate for a few minutes to see whether it sets. If it is too runny, return to the heat stirring frequently for a further 5–10 minutes or until it thickens.

Pour into individual dishes and garnish with flaked almonds, silver leaf (if using) and drizzle with saffron milk. Serve hot or cold. To make it more creamy add a little single cream before serving.

Chocolatey Elaichi Tart

Chocolate and Cardamom Tart

For the sweet pastry

125 g (4 oz) plain flour

A pinch of salt

25 g (1 oz) medium or coarse
  grain semolina

60 g (2½ oz) butter, chilled

50 g (2 oz) icing sugar, sifted

1 small egg

For the filling

300 ml (½ pint) double cream

50 ml (2 fl oz) whole milk

A few saffron threads

200 g (7 oz) dark chocolate
  (70% cocoa solids), broken
  into pieces

2 eggs, separated

4 tablespoons caster sugar

SERVES 4–6

FROM YOUR SPICE BOX

WHOLE SPICES

5 cardamom pods

To decorate

Cocoa powder, for dusting

25 g (1 oz) pistachios, chopped

25 g (1 oz) sliced almonds,
  toasted

To make the pastry, mix the flour and salt in a large bowl and add the semolina. Rub in the chilled butter to make a fine crumb texture.

Add the icing sugar, mix in the egg and combine to form a ball. Work as little as possible with the pastry, or it will end up being very tough. Flatten the pastry slightly, wrap in cling film and chill for 30 minutes.

Preheat the oven to 180°C/350°F/Gas mark 4.

Unwrap the dough and on a lightly floured surface, roll it out as thin as possible. Use the pastry to line a 23 cm (9 inch) tart tin and trim the edges. Line with baking paper and fill with baking beans. Bake blind for 20 minutes in the preheated oven then remove the beans and baking paper and bake for a further 5 minutes.

To make the filling, bring the cream and milk to the boil in a saucepan and add the whole spice and saffron. Place cling film over the top of the saucepan and infuse the spices for 10 minutes. Strain to remove the spices.

Melt the chocolate in a bowl set over a saucepan of simmering water – taking care that the bowl does not touch the water. Add this to the cream. Mix well and set aside for 10 minutes to cool.

Beat the egg yolks with 2 tablespoons of the sugar until light and creamy. Fold the creamy mixture into the chocolate mixture. Beat the egg whites in another bowl and slowly add the remaining sugar. Fold this into the chocolate mixture with a metal spoon and pour into the pastry shell.

Bake in the preheated oven for 12 minutes until slightly cracked around the edge, lightly raised and with a slight wobble to the centre. Remove from the oven and leave to cool. Dust the top of the tart with cocoa powder and decorate with pistachios and sliced almonds.

This tart is perfect for chocolate lovers, with its creamy filling enriched with warm cardamom and saffron flavours.

Sooji Halva

Semolina Halva

150 g (5 oz) caster sugar

A few saffron threads

250 g (8 oz) medium or coarse grain semolina

50 ml (2 fl oz) milk

475 ml (16 fl oz) boiling water

150 g (5 oz) ghee

25 g (1 oz) sliced almonds, roughly chopped

25 g (1 oz) toasted pistachio nuts

SERVES 4

FROM YOUR SPICE BOX

WHOLE SPICES

A good pinch of cardamom seeds, finely crushed

Dissolve the sugar in 50 ml (2 fl oz) of the boiling water to make a sugar syrup. Add the whole spices and saffron and leave to infuse for 10 minutes.

Meanwhile, heat a large wok or frying pan over a high heat and add the semolina. Stir continuously as it browns. The semolina will from a yellow to light brown colour if you have been stirring evenly.

Turn down the heat, make a well in the centre of the granules and add the milk and remaining boiling water. Mix thoroughly. The semolina will start to boil and form a thick broth-style mixture in about 2–3 minutes. It should become a thick viscous mixture that doesn't fall off the wooden spoon easily.

Take the pan off the heat, add the ghee and stir until it has completely melted and combined with the semolina.

Add the sugar syrup to the semolina and mix well. Return to the heat for 1 minute, pour into individual bowls and add the chopped nuts before serving. Serve with a drizzle of single cream or on its own.

For us, a hot bowl of this melt-in-the-mouth halva was always welcome on a wintery day.

Ras Malai

Paneer in a Sweet Creamy Sauce

200 g (7 oz) home-made
  paneer (see page 11)
150 g (5 oz) caster sugar, plus
  3 teaspoons
½ teaspoon baking powder
15 g (½ oz) sliced almonds,
  toasted
15 g (½ oz) pistachios, halved

For the milk sauce
750 ml (1¼ pints) whole milk
A good pinch of saffron threads
2½ tablespoons caster sugar

MAKES ABOUT 12

FROM YOUR SPICE BOX
WHOLE SPICES
5 cardamom pods, 3 finely
  crushed, and 2 pods
  discarded and seeds ground

Mash the paneer in a bowl and mix it with the 3 teaspoons of caster sugar and the baking powder in a bowl. Knead well, shape into 12 small balls and then slightly flatten them.

To make a syrup, combine the remaining sugar with the 3 crushed cardamom pods and 1 litre (1¾ pints) water in a large shallow saucepan and heat slowly until the sugar is dissolved.

Put the paneer balls in the sugar syrup and simmer carefully for 10 minutes. The paneer balls should be spongy in appearance. Remove from the heat and set aside.

To make the milk sauce, bring the milk to the boil in a saucepan with the saffron threads and keep it simmering for 20–25 minutes, stirring to prevent the milk from burning at the bottom. When the milk has reduced by about half, add the sugar and stir well. Remove from the heat.

Gently squeeze some of the sugary liquid out of each of the spongy paneer balls in turn between two spoons. Place the paneer balls into the milk sauce and leave to cool.

Add the ground cardamom, sliced almonds and pistachios and cover. Refrigerate until ready to serve and serve chilled.

Gulab Jamun

Sweet Milk Dumplings in Rose Syrup

For the dumplings

100 g (3½ oz) full-cream milk
  powder
1½ tablespoons ghee or
  unsalted butter
25 g (1 oz) plain flour
15 g (½ oz) ground semolina
¼ teaspoon baking powder
5 tablespoons milk, to bind

For the rose syrup

250 g (8 oz) sugar
6–8 saffron threads
2–3 drops of rose water

To finish

Edible silver leaf, to decorate
  (optional)

MAKES 12 DUMPLINGS

FROM YOUR SPICE BOX
WHOLE SPICES

3 cardamon pods, crushed,
  pods discarded and seeds
  ground

Mix together all of the dumpling ingredients including the cardamom to form a soft dough in a large bowl. Knead for 4–5 minutes, shape into a ball, cover and leave to rest for 30 minutes.

To make the syrup, heat a saucepan over a medium heat. Add the sugar to 500 ml (17 fl oz) water and bring to the boil, stirring continuously, until it becomes just sticky – you can test a little between your fingers.

Remove the pan from the heat, stir in the saffron and rose water and set aside.

If the dough is too dry add a little more milk and knead well. Shape the dough into balls the size of a walnut, making sure that each ball is smooth with no cracks.

Heat the ghee or unsalted butter in a large wok-style frying pan over a medium heat. When hot, reduce the heat, wait a few minutes then add the dumplings – they should float to the top and double their size.

Fry the dumplings until golden brown, remove with a slotted spoon and put straight into the warm rose syrup and continue to simmer gently for 2 minutes. Before serving, decorate with edible silver leaf (if using). Serve warm with a little syrup or with Mango Ice Cream (page 167).

This is an easy dessert to make for a dinner party as it can be made the day before and simply warmed through before serving.

Zafran Nankhatai
Semolina Saffron Biscuits

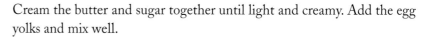

200 g (7 oz) unsalted butter
100 g (3½ oz) caster sugar
2 egg yolks
½ teaspoon baking powder
60 g (2½ oz) medium or coarse grain semolina
250 g (8 oz) plain flour
4–5 saffron threads, lightly crushed
¼ teaspoon nutmeg
Unsalted flaked pistachios, to finish

MAKES ABOUT 25 BISCUITS

FROM YOUR SPICE BOX
WHOLE SPICES
2 cardamom pods, crushed, pods discarded and seeds ground

Cream the butter and sugar together until light and creamy. Add the egg yolks and mix well.

Stir in the rest of the ingredients, except the pistachios, and mix until you have a smooth, soft dough. Alternatively, use an electric mixer. Cover and leave to rest for about 40–45 minutes.

Preheat the oven to 200°C/400°F/Gas mark 6.

Shape the dough in the palms of your hands to form about 25 small balls each about the size of a walnut. Flatten a little and make an indent in the middle of each.

Press a few flakes of pistachio into the middle of each indent and place the biscuits on a baking sheet lined with non-stick baking paper, leaving a space between each one.

Bake in the preheated oven on the middle shelf for 10 minutes. Do not over cook – the biscuits should be pale in colour not golden.

Leave to cool before storing in an airtight container.

Whenever we visited our grandmother we would all make these light melt-in-the-mouth biscuits together. It became a ritual watching them bake in the clay oven. They are easy to make and perfect with a mug of tea.

Kashmiri Mewa Pulao

Kashmiri Sweet Rice with Dried Fruits

40 g (1½ oz) unsalted cashews

300 g (10 oz) basmati rice

½ tablespoon black peppercorns

125 g (4 oz) unsalted butter

40 g (1½ oz) dried dates

40 g (1½ oz) blanched
  almonds

40 g (1½ oz) sultanas

½ teaspoon saffron threads
  soaked in 3 tablespoons warm
  milk

75 g (3 oz) caster sugar

Large pinch of ground nutmeg

SERVES 6–8

FROM YOUR SPICE BOX

WHOLE SPICES

4 cm (1½ inch) cinnamon stick

4 cloves

6 cardamom pods, crushed

Soak the cashews in just enough hot water to cover them for 15 minutes.

Gently wash the rice in a sieve under running water cold water until the water runs clear.

In a small piece of muslin, tie together the peppercorns and the whole spices to make a parcel.

Heat the butter in a heavy-based saucepan (this must be heavy-based with a good sealing lid) over a low–medium heat and add the whole spices tied in the muslin, the nuts and dried fruits. Stir constantly until the nuts and dried fruits are golden brown.

Add the drained rice and the saffron milk and stir. Add the sugar and nutmeg and continue to stir for at least 10 minutes, gently turning the rice mixture.

Add 450 ml (¾ pint) water, boil for 5 minutes over a medium heat then reduce the heat to the lowest setting. Place some foil over the top of the saucepan to make a tight seal and then put the lid on and leave to cook for 30–40 minutes. Stand the saucepan on a frying pan to make sure the rice does not burn. When it is cooked the rice should be soft and separated.

Serve warm as a dessert or teatime snack.

Himalayan Phaal Aur Shrikand

Himalayan Fruit Salad and Creamy Saffron Yogurt

For the sauce (shrikand)

1 litre (1¾ pints) thick-set natural yogurt

¼ teaspoon saffron threads, soaked in 4 teaspoons warm milk

5–6 tablespoons caster sugar

1 apricot, chopped (optional)

For the fruits

150 g (5 oz) strawberries, hulled and cut in half

150 g (5 oz) raspberries

160 g (5½ oz) blueberries

16 green grapes

12 red cherries, stoned and cut in half

1 peach, stoned and cut into segments

¼ cantaloupe melon, peeled and cut into cubes

1 apricot, skinned and diced (optional)

Juice of ½ lime

SERVES 4

FROM YOUR SPICE BOX

WHOLE SPICES

4 cardamom pods, finely crushed

To finish

15 g (½ oz) toasted flaked almonds

Pomegranate seeds

Line a sieve with a muslin or very thin cloth and pour the yogurt into it. Drain for at least 6 hours or overnight in the fridge.

Discard the strained liquid and tip the thick, solid yogurt into a bowl. Add the saffron milk, crushed cardamom and sugar. Whisk to a smooth consistency and add the chopped apricot (if using).

Wash all of the fruits and place them in a large mixing bowl. Drizzle with lime juice.

Serve in individual dishes with the sauce (shrikand) and sprinkle with toasted flaked almonds and pomegranate seeds.

Aam Ki Kulfi
Mango Ice Cream

1 large mango, peeled and
   stoned
200 ml (7 fl oz) condensed
   milk
175 ml (6 fl oz) whipping
   cream

To finish
Unsalted pistachios, finely
   chopped
Edible silver leaf (optional)
Sliced mango

Ice cream maker, 8–10 kulfi
   moulds or a freezer-proof
   container

SERVES 6-8

FROM YOUR SPICE BOX
WHOLE SPICES
1 cardamom pod, finely
   crushed

Purée the mango flesh in a food processor or blender until smooth. Add the crushed cardamom and the condensed milk to the food processor or blender and blitz for a further 30– 40 seconds. Transfer to a large bowl and set aside.

Whip the cream in a bowl and gently fold into the mango–milk mixture until the colour is uniform again. If using an ice cream maker, follow the manufacturer's instructions. If using kulfi moulds, fill them with the mango mixture, seal and freeze for 6 hours.

If using a freezer-proof container with a lid, pour in the mango mixture, cover and freeze for 30 minutes. Remove the container from the freezer and beat with a whisk for 1–2 minutes to give a smoother consistency to the ice cream. Return to the freezer for another 30 minutes before removing and beating with a whisk for 1–2 minutes. Freeze for a further 6 hours.

Remove the container or kulfi moulds from the freezer and place in the fridge for 15 minutes until ready to eat to soften slightly.

Sprinkle with the finely chopped pistachios and edible silver leaf (if using) and garnish with slices of mango.

Dahi Shahad Aur Dalchini Ice Cream

Honey, Yogurt and Cinnamon Ice Cream

150 ml (¼ pint) milk

150 ml (¼ pint) single cream

1½ tablespoons clear honey

¼ teaspoon cinnamon

A large pinch of saffron threads

3 egg yolks

75 g (3 oz) caster sugar

300 ml (½ pint) natural yogurt

1 teaspoon lemon juice

A few chopped almonds,
   to serve

Ice cream maker or a freezer-
   proof container with a lid

SERVES 4–6

FROM YOUR SPICE BOX
WHOLE SPICES

2 cardamom seeds, finely
   crushed

Heat the milk, cream, honey, cardamom, cinnamon and saffron threads in a saucepan over a medium heat. Stir constantly and remove from the heat before it reaches boiling. Do not let it boil.

In a bowl whisk together the egg yolks and sugar until light and creamy. Pour the milk mixture into the bowl in stages and mix well.

Pour the combined mixture back into the saucepan and return to a low heat, stirring constantly, until the mixture thickens. This should take a few minutes.

Remove from heat, transfer to a bowl and leave to cool in the fridge for about 40–45 minutes. Make sure the mixture is completely cold then stir in the yogurt and lemon juice.

If using an ice cream maker, follow the manufacturer's instructions. Alternatively, pour into a freezer-proof container with a lid and freeze for 1 hour. Remove from the freezer and whisk to break up any crystals (you can do this with an electric whisk).

Do this again after every 45 minutes, at least 3 or 4 times. This makes for a creamier ice cream with no ice crystals.

Remove from the freezer about 20 minutes before serving to soften slightly and serve topped with chopped almonds. Serve with Sweet Rice Flour Pancakes (page 34).

A refreshing end to an Indian meal.

Namkeen Aur Meetha Lassi

Yogurt Shake

500 ml (17 fl oz) natural
yogurt

450 ml (¾ pint) chilled water

½ teaspoon salt (or to taste)

Ice cubes or crushed ice

2–3 small mint leaves, to finish

SERVES 4

FROM YOUR SPICE BOX

WHOLE SPICES

½ teaspoon (1 spice spoon)
cumin seeds

Heat a small frying pan over a medium heat and dry roast the cumin seeds for 30 seconds until the seeds turn dark brown. When cool, coarsely grind the toasted cumin seeds using a pestle and mortar. Reserve a pinch of the dry roasted cumin to use as a garnish.

Blend the yogurt, water, salt and dry roasted spice together. Before serving, stir well and pour into tall glasses with ice. Garnish with mint leaves and some of the reserved dry roasted cumin.

Note: to make a sweet lassi, replace the salt, whole spice and mint leaves with 2 tablespoons caster sugar.

Nothing would quench our thirst on a hot Himalayan day as well as this refreshing lassi.

Aam ki Lassi
Mango Yogurt Shake

2 large ripe mangoes, peeled
  and stoned
Pinch of salt
450 ml (¾ pint) chilled milk
750 ml (1¼ pints) natural
  yogurt
5 teaspoons caster sugar
Ice cubes or crushed ice

SERVES 4

FROM YOUR SPICE BOX
WHOLE SPICES
1 cardamom pod, finely
  crushed

Purée the mango in a food processor or blender and pour into a mesh sieve with the salt.

Using the back of a wooden spoon, push the purée through and collect the thick juice. Discard the fibres that collect in the sieve.

Combine the juice with the whole spice and remaining ingredients except the ice, using a whisk or a food processor or blender until smooth.

Pour into tall glasses leaving space for some crushed ice or cubes. Cover and chill in the fridge for 15 minutes. Before serving, stir well and add the crushed ice or cubes.

A great mid-morning pick-me-up and high in vitamins A and C.

Nimbu Pani

Lime Water

1 litre (1¾ pints) chilled water,
  still or sparkling
4 tablespoons caster sugar
  (or to taste)
Juice of 5 limes, strained
A pinch of freshly ground
  black pepper (optional)
Ice cubes or crushed ice
4 lime slices, to finish

SERVES 4

Pour approximately half the quantity of the measured water into a jug and add the sugar.

Whisk until the sugar is well dissolved and none of the grains are visible at the bottom of the jug.

Stir in the lime juice and add the remainder of the water with a pinch of pepper (if using). Serve chilled with ice and slices of lime.

A cooling drink with a zingy citrus kick that can also be made with lemons.

Mugal Chai

Green Tea with Cinnamon and Cardamom

2–3 saffron threads crushed

2 teaspoons loose leaf green tea

6 teaspoons granulated sugar
 (or to taste)

Toasted, flaked almonds, to
 finish

SERVES 4

FROM YOUR SPICE BOX

WHOLE SPICES

4 cardamom pods, crushed

4 cm (1½ inch) cinnamon stick

Heat 750 ml (1¼ pints) water in a saucepan over a high heat. When it comes to a boil add the whole spices including the saffron, tea leaves and sugar. Continue to boil for 30 seconds.

Remove from the heat, cover and leave for 2 minutes. Strain the tea into cups and sprinkle with flaked almonds.

We have all been drinking this tea since we were little. It is a good antioxidant and also very comforting if you have a cold.

Index